Contents

Acknowledgements

In writing this book, I have incurred too many debts of gratitude to count. First and foremost, to the wonderful Kate O'Regan, whose steadfast support and sage insights have made this book possible, and the great team at the Bonavero Institute of Human Rights, University of Oxford. Zoe Davis-Heaney and Sarah Norman, especially, for their administrative nous and good humour, and Annelen Micus and Liora Lazarus for their enthusiasm and advice. Many thanks also go to colleagues in the Centre for Socio-Legal Studies, Department of Politics and International Relations, and the Faculty of Law, as well as staff at the Bodleian Library.

My deepest thanks to the Legal Education Foundation, who provided generous financial support, under the strong leadership of Matthew Smerdon, and the indefatigable Director of Research, Natalie Byrom.

I have benefited from many discussions over the years on access to justice and class actions, most notably with Andrew Higgins, who always offers gems of wisdom over lunches at Mansfield College, and many others, including Isabella Bakker, Stephen Gill, Trevor Farrow, Regina Kiener, John Waller, Chris Stone, Suzanne Chiodo, Jeremias and Abi Adams-Prassl, Richard Martin and Mansfield's two principals in my time, Helen Mountfield and Helena Kennedy.

Many people gave their time and thoughts to be interviewed for this project, often very senior stakeholders in England and Wales with very busy schedules, despite knowing that they would remain anonymous and no one would know their efforts. I am thankful to all of them.

The team at Bristol University Press – particularly Helen Davis and Freya Trand – have been a delight to work with in the production of this book. An author could not ask for a more supportive and understanding team.

Finally, I owe thanks to my family and friends for their endless patience and support. Above all, to Moa, who always nods along to whatever has got my goat on any given day.

Preface

This book has arisen out of a research project I have undertaken as a postdoctoral research fellow at the Bonavero Institute of Human Rights, University of Oxford, funded by the Legal Education Foundation. A key insight that I garnered from interviews with civil justice stakeholders as part of my empirical data collection was the relative lack of knowledge about class actions in England and Wales. For some, this was a result of the perceived neglect of civil procedure in English universities in contrast to places like Australia, Canada and the United States, where it is more foundational to legal education. Others took a more socio-cultural perspective, observing that even among academics, let alone the proverbial person on the street, much knowledge about class actions comes from popular media, whether television and film or the mainstream news, which has contributed to the impoverished understanding of the legal vehicle. Whichever the cause(s), a common refrain among stakeholders was that one of the major challenges for reform in the area is this fundamental lack of knowledge. One senior stakeholder went so far as to suggest that, at first instance, nothing would do more for collective access to justice than tackling this gap. It is my hope, then, that a book of this nature will be useful for those seeking to learn more about class actions and their benefits for access to justice. This approach aligns well with the growing recognition that 'access to justice' research needs to be more self-reflexive and incorporate its own central tenets: the research itself needs to be accessible. Too often this is ironically not the case. That is why I have chosen this format, and I have sought, to the best of my ability, to write in a clear and accessible manner. Given the somewhat technical language of the subject matter, this has at times proven to be a challenge, but I hope that a good balance has been struck between appealing to readers with previous familiarity and those who may not know much about the topic at hand.

Michael Molavi
Oxford, June 2020

ONE

Collective Access to Justice

In England and Wales today, calls for increasing access to justice are omnipresent. Justice stakeholders have observed at length that the capacity of people to access justice is paramount in a democracy governed by the rule of law. The purview of the current access to justice agenda has thus been quite broad, covering everything from the rise in litigants-in-person – that is, individuals who are representing themselves as opposed to being represented by legal professionals – to the digital modernization of Her Majesty's Courts and Tribunals Service through the use of new technology and the move to online courts and tribunals. Despite this breadth, however, and the commitment of stakeholders to find innovative ways of addressing the accessibility gaps in the justice system, a consistent unifying theme that runs throughout this commitment has been its individuated focus. Research and reform in access to justice has tended to be guided by the belief that justiciable problems affect individuals as private persons and must therefore be addressed through individuated solutions, typically geared at delivering outcomes, whether through public courts or, increasingly, through the private fora of alternative dispute resolution mechanisms such as arbitration and mediation. This book seeks to advance this agenda by exploring the role of class actions in promoting collective access to justice.

In late modern societies, groups are seeking justice for mass harms that are as diverse as they are widespread: from mass data breaches affecting millions and mass injuries arising out of faulty products to mass labour disputes in the gig economy and mass health impairment from toxic environmental pollution. Such claims are often impractical or irrational to pursue individually against well-resourced opponents, often transnational corporations. The advantages enjoyed by such 'repeat players' against 'one-shotters', to invoke the classic thesis, has led Marc Galanter to identify the modern class action as a procedure capable of addressing the power imbalances and resource disparities on display in such cases.[1] Galanter goes on to observe that the 'intensity of opposition to class action legislation ... indicates the "haves" own estimation of the relative strategic impact' of the procedure.[2] The diffuse and fragmented nature of many such harms typically leaves a disorganized mass of people who require some catalyzing entity – such as experienced lawyers or NGOs – to synthesize and advance their claims. In such cases, then, aggregating individual claims into a collective procedure can promote an equality of arms between parties and facilitate access to justice for groups as a whole.

The broader social and political context is also worth noting. Such collective procedures are particularly needed in light of the juridification of the social sphere since the creation of the modern welfare state and the expansion of legal regulation in the post-war period.[3] This proliferation has given rise to

---

[1] M. Galanter, 'Why the "Haves" Come Out Ahead: Speculations on the Limits of Legal Change' (1974) 9 *Law and Society Review* 95, 97.

[2] ibid at 97.

[3] Juridification as a juridico-political process dates to the advent of the modern nation state, as Habermas observes, and can be conceptualized in successive stages, with its contemporary form of the increasing legalization of social structures, conditions and relations being a major theme in political debates since the 1980s. This rich literature is perhaps best exemplified in Habermas's treatment of the subject in *The Theory of Communicative Action, Volume 2: Lifeworld and System* (Cambridge: Polity,

legitimate concerns about the capacity of people to navigate the 'law-thick' worlds in which they find themselves. Although access to justice has long been heralded as one of the great pillars of the post-war British welfare state, empowering vulnerable people to enforce their rights and protect their interests takes on heightened significance in this context. In short, the central place of law in the modern state and its expansion into practically every facet of society now means that securing access to justice is no longer only a matter of actualizing a long-standing normative ideal (rooted in the Magna Carta) but is increasingly a practical requirement for people to be able to navigate this novel juridical setting and benefit from the protection of the law.[4]

This entails, as this book argues, both individual and collective forms of legal empowerment and accessibility. Although the former has a long-standing history and remains a permanent fixture in legal reform and research agendas, the latter has been relatively neglected in England and Wales. Yet the importance of collective access to justice was not lost on the early pioneers in the field. By the middle of the 20th century, most liberal democracies had recognized the importance of ensuring effective, rather than merely formal, access to justice for their citizens. Although many democracies had already introduced limited regimes of accessibility promotion, particularly for criminal justice proceedings, including England and Wales

---

1987). See also G. Teubner (ed), *Juridification of Social Spheres* (Berlin: de Gruyter, 1987); R.M. Unger, *Law in Modern Society* (New York, NY: The Free Press, 1976); R. Cotterrell, *The Sociology of Law: An Introduction* (London: Butterworths, 1992); B. de Sousa Santos, *Towards a New Legal Common Sense* (London: Butterworths, 2002).

[4] The term 'access to justice' can be traced to the 19th century, although its conceptual origin in the Magna Carta (1215) is clear: 'To no one will we sell, to no one will we refuse or deny, right or justice.' The term, however, was popularized in the 1970s. See A. Paterson, *Lawyers and the Public Good: Democracy in Action?* (The Hamlyn Lectures) (Cambridge: Cambridge University Press, 2011).

with, for example, the Poor Prisoners' Defence Act and the Criminal Appeal Act 1907 – the former only applying where a prisoner was deemed to have a defence and the latter extending to murder appeals and other select criminal appeals – it was only in the post-war milieu that the newly established welfare states in Europe began introducing comprehensive civil justice regimes. This commitment was echoed in the 1960s in North America, where the Civil Rights Movement and progressive liberal legal actors increasingly sought access to the courts to achieve their social and political objectives. One notable facet of this development was the recognition of the collective nature of many of these claims and the need for a collective claims-making vehicle for their pursuit. The procedural innovation of the modern class action, introduced in the United States with the revised Rule 23 of the Federal Rules of Civil Procedure in 1966, must be viewed in this historical context of increasing legal empowerment.

Waves of access to justice

To borrow the 'waves' metaphor from the cornerstone of 20th-century scholarship in access to justice, the multi-volume research project initiated in the 1970s by Mauro Cappelletti and Bryant Garth, the *Florence Access to Justice Project* ('Florence Project'), research and reforms can be broadly categorized in successive waves.[5] While there is a chronology in the waves insofar as each occurs before the one that follows, they are not confined to discrete periods of development, but are rather ongoing processes.

The First Wave is characterized by an emphasis on legal aid regimes designed to mitigate the costs of court proceedings for

---

[5] M. Cappelletti and B. Garth (eds), *Access to Justice – A World Survey* (Alphen aan den Rijn: Sijthoff and Noordhoff, 1978). The project was commenced in 1973 and completed in 1977–8.

the poor. The focus here is the importance of judicare systems in which individuals with insufficient economic resources (who satisfy state qualification criteria) are provided with state-funded legal services.[6] In England and Wales this took the form of the 1949 Legal Aid and Advice Act, implemented by the Labour government of Clement Attlee. The ideal that animates such public expenditure is that nobody should be denied the services of a lawyer – and the justice that ostensibly flows from this service – due to their diminished economic standing. Or even more aspirationally: that low-income individuals would benefit from the same quality of service that they would otherwise have received if they had the means to pay for their own lawyer – the only difference being that it is the state that assumes the cost rather than the individual, with all else remaining equal.[7] The common reductive understanding of 'access to justice' to mean simply 'legal aid' can be rooted to these origins, and although some commentators continue to use the two terms interchangeably, successive waves in the movement have expanded the scope of the concept in promising directions.

Recognizing that the legal aid models of the First Wave – which remain the dominant approach – were too individualistic and did not address diffuse and collective harms, the Second Wave of reforms sought to address these concerns by focusing on the justiciable problems of groups of similarly situated individuals or cohesive collectives. As Cappelletti and Garth observe, the Second Wave sought to expand the prevailing 'individualistic vision'[8] of access to justice towards a 'social,

---

[6]   ibid at 24–7. Much debate has been waged on the qualification criteria and means-testing standards, and, more theoretically, about the legitimacy of such testing. For policy stakeholders, a major consideration has been the exclusion of the unmet legal needs of those who do not qualify for legal aid, notably the 'missing middle' – middle income earners who cannot afford legal services but do not qualify for legal aid who are, in effect, paying in taxes for a service that they need and cannot access.

[7]   ibid at 25.

[8]   ibid at 36.

collective conception'.[9] Given the largely individualistic legal paradigms of liberal democracies, this involved the introduction of procedural reforms to allow for collective or aggregated claims-making. Perhaps the most effective, and certainly the most controversial, form that this type of collective procedure has taken is the class action lawsuit.

In the early 1980s, a Third Wave of reforms grew in popularity as policymakers sought to expand the very basis of justice delivery from an emphasis on formal court procedures to private dispute resolution, usually grouped under the umbrella term of alternative dispute resolution mechanisms (ADR). Budgetary constraints and restrictions in social expenditures, coupled with increasing costs associated with pursuing claims in the formal court system, precipitated this shift towards privatization through fora such as arbitration and mediation. The ADR movement steadily gained momentum in the 1990s where, in England and Wales, the new landscape found a strong ally in Lord Woolf, who promoted the shift in 1996 in the Final Report of his influential review of access to justice, and it found expression in the new Civil Procedure Rules and the Access to Justice Act 1999.[10] One of the defining features of this wave has been its emphasis on treating courts as the fora of last resort for accessing justice.

Although the effectiveness of ADR has been incontrovertible in practical terms, which is to say, as a cost-effective and expeditious option that lessens the burden on the public purse and preserves scarce judicial resources, a rich critical literature has developed that questions the quality of justice that such mechanisms deliver and the power imbalances, procedural deficiencies and broader social and democratic ramifications of

---

[9] ibid.

[10] Rt Hon. Lord Woolf, *Access to Justice, Interim Report* (Lord Chancellor's Department, 1995); Rt Hon. Lord Woolf, *Final Report to the Lord Chancellor on the Civil Justice System in England and Wales* (HMSO, July 1996).

such privatization.[11] For our purposes, critics of class actions have often advocated for ADR mechanisms in place of formal legal action, particularly in the consumer and employment context.[12] One notable development of the Third Wave of reforms has been the advent of mandatory arbitration clauses. This is a major problem in the United States, in contrast to the negative approach to them in most European jurisdictions, including England and Wales. The plain objective of such clauses is the diversion of justiciable problems out of the public court system and into private arbitration, where power imbalances can be capitalized upon by actors who may otherwise be subject to litigation. This has been particularly controversial in the context of consumer and employment contracts whereby individuals are effectively prevented from participating in class actions (often via explicit provisions). Another, distinctly American, development worth noting has been the advent of class arbitration as a form of dispute resolution, which can be broadly described as a combination of private arbitration and traditional class actions.[13] Whereas arbitration has historically

---

[11] An influential account of some criticisms of ADR in the context of England and Wales can be found in H. Genn, *Judging Civil Justice* (The Hamlyn Lectures) (Cambridge: Cambridge University Press, 2010). See also T.C.W. Farrow, *Civil Justice, Privatization and Democracy* (Toronto: University of Toronto Press, 2014).

[12] See, eg, C. Hodges, *Delivering Dispute Resolution: A Holistic Review of Models in England and Wales* (Oxford: Beck Hart Nomos, 2019); C. Hodges and S. Voet, *Delivering Collective Redress: New Technologies* (Oxford: Beck Hart Nomos, 2019).

[13] As part of a broader curtailment of mass litigation in the United States, even class arbitration has come under criticism and to varying degrees been curtailed. See, eg, G. Vairo, 'Is the Class Action Really Dead? Is that Good or Bad for Class Members?' (2014) 64 *Emory Law Journal* 477–529. Class arbitration in the United States has its origins in the early 1980s but gained increased momentum following *Green Tree Financial Corp. v Bazzle* [2003] 539 US 444, wherein the United States Supreme Court 'implicitly approved the procedure'.

been a bilateral process (or, at any rate, has tended to involve a limited number of parties), class arbitration has a representative character and may involve significantly more parties, rather like traditional class proceedings. Yet the most problematic, and certainly most far-reaching, facet of the Third Wave has been ideological. The ADR movement has coalesced around a discernible anti-litigation narrative, arguing that civil justice in the late 20th century suffers from both 'too little access' and 'too much litigation'.[14] It is beyond the scope of this book to engage more fully with this ideological critique, but as Judith Resnik, Deborah Hensler, Hazel Genn, Marc Galanter and numerous other leading scholars have observed, in addition to the disputable outcomes for justice-seekers that such mechanisms provide, the anti-litigation impetus and rhetoric of this wave belies an impoverished understanding of the social importance of civil justice and its public role in a healthy democratic polity.

Starting in the 1990s, a Fourth Wave in research and reforms began to become discernible. This wave took on board the insights of socio-legal scholarship at the time that emphasized the importance of preventative approaches and conflict avoidance. This was reflected in an expansive understanding of the concept of access to justice to include the dual features of accessibility promotion, its traditional domain, with injustice prevention. The Fourth Wave thinking has been popularly encapsulated with a metaphor culled from risk management studies: 'Most people would surely prefer a fence at the top of the cliff rather than an ambulance at the bottom (no matter how swift or well-equipped).'[15] While it is clearly a matter of common sense that people would prefer to avoid legal problems altogether – we can recall, for instance, 19th-century adages such as 'an ounce of prevention is worth a pound of cure' – concerns remain about the extent to which many justiciable

---

[14] Genn (n 11) at 53.
[15] R. Susskind, *The End of Lawyers? Rethinking the Nature of Legal Services* (Oxford: Oxford University Press, 2010) at 231.

problems are avoidable in the first place through individual decision-making and behavioural changes. Such concerns are especially pronounced for problems that are collective in nature, such as environmental pollution, anti-competitive conduct by global cartels, mass discriminatory practices by employers and the like. At an individual level, too, empirical studies have shown that 'people whose social position is near the bottom of an unequal structure will be less likely to take actions that might protect or further their own interests, whether those actions involve seeking information or advice'.[16]

Finally, a Fifth Wave has been discernible since the early 2000s which has sought to expand the scope of the concept into areas of social life that have not traditionally been viewed as being part of the purview of the 'access to justice' movement. This conceptual progression has been described by Galanter as reflecting the essential feature of justice as a 'fluid, moving, and labile thing',[17] which implies that the normative goal of 'access to justice', by extension, must be a constantly 'moving frontier'.[18] As such, policy reforms that focus exclusively on formal legal channels have started to be viewed as insufficient measures for dealing with the multi-dimensionality of justiciable problems (or 'unmet legal needs') as these exist in a social ecosystem. Perhaps the major growth area of Fifth Wave development has been grounded on appreciating the role of effective legal intervention in mitigating health inequalities.[19]

---

[16] R. Sandefur, 'The Importance of Doing Nothing: Everyday Problems and Responses of Inaction' in P. Pleasance, A. Buck and N. Balmer (eds), *Transforming Lives: Law and Social Process* (London: HMSO, 2007) at 117.

[17] M. Galanter, 'Access to Justice as a Moving Frontier' in J. Bass, W.A. Bogart and F.H. Zemans (eds), *Access to Justice for a New Century: The Way Forward* (Toronto: Law Society of Upper Canada, 2005) at 147–53.

[18] ibid.

[19] In England and Wales this has been a major focus of Genn's recent work. See, eg, H. Genn, 'When Law Is Good for Your Health: Mitigating the Social Determinants of Health through Access to Justice' (2019) 72(1) *Current Legal Problems* 159–202.

What is clear, then, from this brief review, is that the 'access to justice' movement has undergone several changes and developed in different, sometimes conflicting, directions since the mid-20th century. At root, however, remains the capacity of people to benefit from the protection that the law can offer. One of the goals of this book is to explore the ways in which this protection is lacking for groups in the current civil justice landscape in England and Wales, and to examine, in so doing, the role that a collective claims-making vehicle such as the class action can play in addressing these accessibility gaps.

What is a class action?

There is perhaps no civil procedure that has garnered as much attention in recent decades, yet one might be forgiven for not having a clear answer to this relatively straightforward question. Mass media headlines seem to describe most legal cases involving some form of collective redress as class actions, leaving the average reader bewildered by the sheer variety of mechanisms that are labelled as such. The term does appear to be used as a synonym for 'collective redress mechanism' in common parlance, which contributes to the muddied water of the debate.[20] Before anything else, then, we would do well to clarify what we are talking about when we talk about class actions.

The ideal form that a class action can take (and a workable definition) is a trans-substantive procedure that allows for a representative claimant or body (ideally both should be allowed) to advance a claim on behalf of any number of similarly situated

---

[20] For an overview of such mechanisms, see, eg, R. Mulheron, *The Class Action in Common Law Legal Systems: A Comparative Perspective* (Oxford: Hart Publishing, 2004); C. Hodges, *Multi-Party Actions* (Oxford: Oxford University Press, 2001); E. Lein, D. Fairgrieve, M.O. Crespo and V. Smith (eds), *Collective Redress in Europe – Why and How?* (London: British Institute of International and Comparative Law, 2015).

individuals who have not opted out of the proceeding, preferably in a regime that incentivizes the key enablers, such as lawyers and funders, to provide financing for the litigation (and potentially also to assume the risks).[21] The person bringing the claim on behalf of the similarly situated individuals is referred to as the 'representative claimant', and those individuals are collectively referred to as the 'class'. Although the criteria to be met for a proceeding to qualify as a class action, usually through a pre-trial certification stage, vary across regimes, a standard qualification criterion is that there must be sufficient commonality in the raised facts; which is to say, the claim must be based on common issues that have arisen out of the same or similar wrong(s) as those of the representative claimant. Importantly, the class members are nearly always absent from the proceeding and they are bound by the outcome, although they may, on individual bases, choose to withdraw, in which case they can formally do so (before the relevant deadline).

---

[21] Rachael Mulheron has offered the following working definition:

> A class action is a legal procedure which enables the claims (or part of the claims) of a number of persons against the same defendant to be determined in one suit. In a class action, one or more persons ('representative claimant') may sue on his or her own behalf and on behalf of a number of other persons ('the class') who have a claim to a remedy for the same or similar alleged wrong to that pursued by the representative claimant, and who have claims that share questions of law or fact in common with those of the representative claimant ('common issues'). Only the representative claimant is a party to the action. The class members are not usually identified as individual parties but are merely described. Should they not wish to participate, class members are permitted to opt-out of the class action in the time and manner prescribed. Unless they opt-out, class members are bound by the outcome of the litigation on the common issues, whether favourable or adverse to the class, although they do not, for the most part, take any active part in that litigation.

Mulheron (n 20) at 3.

This is what it means to 'opt out' of the action, and this is the type of mechanism that is being described when the term 'opt-out class action' is used – the inverse of this arrangement, whereby each class member must sign up to the proceeding, or 'opt in', has also been widely considered by law reform bodies. The 'opt-out' class action is, in short, the most robust form of collective mechanism and the form that has attracted the most attention globally. When this book speaks of class actions, this is the procedure that is being spoken about.

In England and Wales the procedure that is commonly discussed when the topic of class actions arises is the Group Litigation Order (GLO). The GLO is, however, a case management tool. It is used when claimants file individual proceedings, which are subsequently grouped into a single action and case managed by the court. The other procedure that is often identified as a class action is the representative rule, which originates in equity. This action is based on the long-standing rule that allows a representative claimant to pursue a proceeding on behalf of a group of two or more individuals who share the 'same interest' in the claim.[22] We will return to both of these in greater detail throughout the book. There are, of course, a host of other options that allow for grouped or representative proceedings and that have, by extension, been identified as class actions, including test actions, where a single proceeding is advanced in order to determine a point of law or fact that will establish a precedent for others with the same or similar

---

[22] Notably, John Sorabji has previously suggested that the representative action can be used by the court to develop a modern class action. See J. Sorabji, 'The Hidden Class Action in English Civil Procedure' (2009) 28(4) *Civil Justice Quarterly* 498; Civil Justice Council, *Improving Access to Justice through Collective Actions: Final Report (A Series of Recommendations to the Lord Chancellor)* (2008); See also R. Mulheron, 'From Representative Rule to Class Action: Steps Rather than Leaps' (2005) 24 *Civil Justice Quarterly* 424; J. Seymour, 'Representative Proceedings and the Future of Multi-Party Actions' (1999) 62 *Modern Law Review* 565.

claims who have either already initiated their own proceedings or who have yet to do so, or who have registered in a group registry awaiting the outcome of the test action. Proceedings that have benefited from being grouped through a joinder or a consolidation – the former referring to grouping two or more parties into a single proceeding so that the issue may be resolved at the same time, and the latter referring to the court uniting proceedings that have already been initiated as a case management tool to ensure consistency and the efficient use of court resources – have also been identified as forms of class proceedings. Most of these options are designed to improve the functioning of courts by avoiding duplication, inconsistent decisions and unnecessary expenditures, rather than promoting accessibility by bringing new legal claims that would not otherwise be brought to the court.

Apart from mislabelling of this sort, the controversy over class actions extends to the use of the term itself, with some commentators seeking to displace the term (and the vehicle itself) in favour of the broader 'collective redress', which is an umbrella term that includes collective litigation, but also includes forms of ADR, ombudsperson services and regulatory redress.[23] Such perspectives often involve a negative view of litigation, largely in line with Third Wave thinking, and seek to promote forms of dispute resolution and redress that do not involve formal legal action. In line with Third Wave thinking, such perspectives often seek to portray litigation in general and class actions specifically as forms of 'old technology', with ADR mechanisms posited as 'new technologies' that offer better returns and increased efficiency through privatized solutions.

---

[23] See, eg, C. Hodges and S. Voet, *Delivering Collective Redress: New Technologies* (Oxford: Hart Publishing, 2018); C. Hodges, *Delivering Dispute Resolution: A Holistic Review of Models in England and Wales* (Oxford: Hart Publishing, 2019).

The debate over class actions, then, can be viewed as a microcosm of the broader debate that has arisen between public and private forms of dispute resolution since the 1980s. Below the surface of the class action debate is a much deeper and far-reaching discussion of the role of law in a democratic state and the extent to which the vehicle assumes functions that have historically been undertaken by public agencies. This was one of the central insights garnered from interviews conducted for this book, from senior members of the judiciary and experienced lawyers from leading firms to members of influential legal reform bodies and NGOs with an interest in collective access to justice. The regulatory function of the class action and its deployment as a policy instrument in a private enforcement regime is clearly an inextricable element of the debate.

Although the uneven reform process in England and Wales will be addressed in greater detail later in this book, for now it suffices to note that the only area where class actions are available (on either an opt-in or opt-out model) is in the Competition Appeal Tribunal.[24] Legislation was introduced in Parliament on 23 January 2014 and came into force on 26 March 2015. In contrast to other regimes, and well-established principles of civil procedure since the 1870s, England and Wales has opted to introduce class actions on a sectoral basis, rather than using a generic or transsubstantive approach. To date, then, claims that are covered in the Competition Appeal Tribunal apart, Lord Woolf's first objective for promoting collective access to justice, as discussed in greater detail later, remains unfulfilled in every other area of law.

---

[24] It is contained through a combination of primary legislation and court rules. Competition Act 1998, ss 47A–49E; Enterprise Act 2002; Competition Appeal Tribunal Rules 2015 (SI 1648/2015), rr 73–98.

Structure of the book

Chapter Two outlines the historical and comparative context of class actions as these have developed since their modern origins in the United States. We recall the longer history of group litigation in England as a way of providing a historical antecedent to contemporary class actions. The chapter traces the development of the United States as a First Generation regime, followed by Canada and Australia as Second Generation regimes. In so doing, the chapter examines recent efforts to institute collective mechanisms and the ways in which these developments have progressed. The chapter focuses on First and Second Generation regimes for comparative insights as these have sustained histories with class actions from which it can be useful to learn in terms of influencing developments in England and Wales, a Third Generation regime. The aim of the chapter is ultimately to illuminate and situate developments in this jurisdiction in broader historical and comparative perspective so that we can have a better sense of the lineage of the vehicle and the extent to which extant developments in England and Wales are falling short of their access to justice potential.

Chapter Three offers a deeper look into reforms in England and Wales. It unpacks the otherwise technical language of class actions as civil procedures to uncover the politics and economic interests involved in reform processes. Debates over class actions have historically been divided along ideological lines, with conservative forces and corporate lobbies seeking to restrict the expansion and delimit the purview of the legal vehicle, and progressive forces (for example human rights groups, trade unions and consumer protection organizations) seeking to introduce and expand their scope. This is partly due to the redistributive feature of class actions and their effectiveness in vindicating the rights of harmed people against largely corporate (and sometimes governmental) misbehaviour on a mass scale. In this chapter, we examine the political and economic interests that have animated discourse and reforms, and the ways in which such interests have perpetuated misconceptions and misinformation about class actions.

Chapter Four examines one of the strongest arguments in favour of the access to justice potential of class actions, which can be found in the rational choice theory of orthodox economics. This economic access to justice framework is based on the recognition that the class action can allow for the pursuit of claims that would otherwise not be pursued by rational actors. In other words, class actions allow for the pursuit of negative value claims – claims in which the value of the claim is outweighed by the costs of its pursuit. By aggregating such claims, class actions facilitate access to justice for those who would otherwise not find vindication for their incurred harms. In such cases, allowing for ideological representatives to advance claims on behalf of harmed groups can contribute towards preventing injustices by deterring misconduct by potential wrongdoers. Indeed, this deterrence function is often cited as a policy objective of class action legislation. Throughout this chapter, we also explore a host of important issues pertaining to the economics of class actions that impact the access to justice that is achieved and achievable through mass litigation, including issues of (third party) funding, (adverse) costs, and disbursements.

The final chapter of the book, Chapter Five, brings together the different veins of our discussion and affirms that the current landscape of collective claims-making leaves a major access to justice gap that demands reform.

TWO

Class Actions in Historical and Comparative Perspective

We might be forgiven for thinking that collective claims-making has arisen out of the massification of modern societies since the Industrial Revolution (1760–1840). In setting the context for the Second Wave of the access to justice movement, Cappelletti and Garth pointed out that 'modern societies are characterised by mass production, mass commerce and consumption, mass urbanization, and mass labour conflicts' and mass litigation is a natural outgrowth of this broader social and economic massification.[1] Critics of the class action, since the origins of its modern incarnation, have also been keen to portray it as a procedural innovation that threatens long-established legal norms and traditions, and perverts justice in the process. But the history is much richer than this perspective suggests.

---

[1] M. Cappelletti, 'Governmental and Private Advocates for the Public Interest in Civil Litigation: A Comparative Study' in M. Cappelletti and J. Weisner (eds), *Access to Justice: Promising Institutions* (Alphen aan den Rijn: Sijthoff and Noordhoff, 1979) at 861.

From medieval origins to the 19th century

The class action has deep roots in group litigation dating back to post-Norman Conquest England.[2] The eminent legal historian Stephen Yeazell has rooted the advent of group litigation to 1199, when a rector of a parish brought a claim against his own parishioners in the court of the Archbishop of Canterbury, seeking customary parochial fees for the burial of the parishioners' deceased.[3] In its earliest incarnation, group litigation involved both defendant and plaintiff groups and thus differed from the contemporary perception of such litigation as empowering vulnerable individuals to band together against powerful wrongdoers (although, in their contemporary form, class actions can also involve both groups). Social group structures pervaded the landscape of the period, and issues that animate our current debate over group litigation, such as the binding nature of such litigation on absent class members or the extent to which representation is compatible with individual rights and entitlements, were left out of the debate.[4]

'It would have made as little sense to medieval lawyers to ask about the litigative standing of communities', observes Yeazell, 'as it would to ask a modern lawyer why individuals can litigate'.[5] Perhaps the most obvious distinction between the two is that the modern class action allows such individuals to form a single litigative entity in order to advance a claim on behalf of all, whereas the medieval incarnation simply allowed an individual to represent a group that already had legal standing. As with any such historical inquiry, it would, of course, be

---

[2] The landmark work of scholarship in class action history is Stephen Yeazell's *From Mediaeval Group Litigation to the Modern Class Action* (New Haven, CT: Yale University Press, 1988).

[3] S.C. Yeazell, 'The Past and Future of Defendant and Settlement Classes in Collective Litigation' (1997) 39 *Arizona Law Review* 688.

[4] ibid at 689.

[5] ibid.

both anachronistic and erroneous to describe the early forays of group litigation in medieval England as class actions in the contemporary usage of the term. Yet the central trait of both the medieval actions and their modern counterparts is the legitimacy of a representative pursuing a claim on behalf of a group of similarly situated individuals, who are typically absent from the proceeding, with the outcome being binding on all.

By the turn of the 18th century, standing for the social group formations (for example villages, communities, parishes and so on) that had previously advanced claims collectively was no longer assumed but had to be determined on a case-by-case basis. Before then, a group was thought to have standing to pursue a case collectively, whereas thereafter a court had to determine whether the group could in fact pursue their case on a collective basis or whether each member of the group had to pursue their case on individual bases.[6] This change arose out of the emergence of the corporation, and more specifically, the grant theory of the corporation, which held, according to Sir Edward Coke, that corporateness was bestowed by the state as a privilege – a privilege which allowed individuals, among other benefits, to sue collectively.[7] The implications of this for group litigation were considerable: if, as the theory held, the power to sue collectively could only be granted by the state, then social groups that had not been granted this power through incorporation could therefore not sue collectively, at least not without special justification.[8] In a sense, then, our current debates over the conditions and criteria under which representative or group litigation can be advanced (for example in the class action setting, the criteria used by courts during the certification stage to determine whether or not a proceeding can be certified as a class action and proceed on that basis) can be traced to this development.[9]

---

[6] ibid at 690.

[7] ibid.

[8] ibid.

[9] ibid.

In the early modern era, however, there remained significant justiciable problems for groups arising out of feudal arrangements, as well as the growth of new collective problems stemming from the radical social and economic upheavals of the 16th and 17th centuries.[10] The procedural rules of the common law courts, which often resulted in numerous individual suits arising out of the same or similar causes of action, were not well equipped for such collective justiciable problems. In contrast to the common law, which approached dispute resolution in a narrow way, holding that it was sufficient to only join as parties those that had direct and immediate legal rights at stake in the matter, equity sought a 'more complete justice',[11] prompting the English Court of Chancery to maintain a rule of compulsory joinder to ensure consistency in decisions and avoid duplicative suits.[12] This was subsequently relaxed to allow for representative actions, holding that one person could bring a

---

[10] ibid.

[11] The contrast between the two approaches is well articulated by F. Calvert in *A Treatise upon the Law Respecting Parties to Suits in Equity* (London: W. Benning, 1847) at 3, who observes:

> In this respect, there is a manifest distinction between the practice of a Court of Law and that of a Court of Equity. A Court of Law decides some one individual question, which is brought before it; a Court of Equity not merely makes a decision to that extent, but also arranges all the rights, which the decision immediately affects.

See also J.A. Kazanjian, 'Class Actions in Canada' (1973) 11 *Osgoode Hall Law Journal* 397.

[12] This rule held that 'all persons materially interested, either legally or beneficially, in the subject matter of a suit, are to be made parties to it, either as plaintiffs or as defendants, however numerous they may be, so that there may be a complete decree which shall bind all', ibid at 400; Ontario Ministry of the Attorney General, Ontario Law Reform Commission, *Report on Class Actions*, vol 1 (Toronto: Queen's Printer, 1982) at 5.

suit on behalf of 'all persons materially interested, either legally or beneficially in the subject matter of the suit'.[13]

The first case in which this revised rule was applied was *Brown v Vermuden* (1676) and offers some insight for our purposes. The case once again involved parishioners: on this occasion, Brown, the Vicar of Worselworth, sought the enforcement of payments from his parishioners as a result of an earlier court judgment. One parishioner, Vermuden, sought to be excluded from any enforcement of payments on the grounds that he was not a party to the earlier action and thus not bound by it. In his decision in favour of Brown, the Lord Chancellor observed that all parishioners must be bound by such decisions, otherwise there would be far too many individual suits for the court to handle.[14] Once again, this was a defendant class, and the principle that absent class members could be bound by a decision was upheld. Unlike a modern opt-out class action, however, in such cases class members could not opt out. This suggests quite a severe arrangement considering that as this was a defendant action, the absent class members did not stand to benefit (as they would from a plaintiff action) but rather stood to be burdened by a court decision.[15]

Fusion of courts of law and equity in 1873

Just as the Court of Chancery adapted in the waning years of feudalism by relaxing its rule of joinder to offer a workable forum for dispute resolution for groups, such as those between parsons and parishioners or lords and tenants, so, too, was the

---

[13] Ontario Law Reform Commission (n 12) at 6.

[14] The Lord Chancellor observed: 'If the Defendant should not be bound, Suits of this Nature, as in the case of Inclosures, Suits against the Inhabitants for Suit to a Mill, and the like, would be infinite and impossible to be ended', Kazanjian (n 11) at 409.

[15] A positive decision in such a case could be construed as a benefit to the defendant class by virtue of the absence of a burden.

rule further relaxed during the 18th century in light of English imperialism and the Industrial Revolution, which generated new forms of collective problems, notably those involving commercial activities, that preceded the advent of the modern limited liability corporation.[16] Indeed, the story of group litigation can be read as a story of juridical adaptation to social and economic changes through the recognition of the types of problems that arise in society and adjusting accordingly to provide adequate rules and mechanisms for their just resolution. In spite of the considerable adaptations that had been made by the mid-18th century, however, the limitations of the prevailing arrangement were obvious. Notably, although the Court of Chancery could provide various forms of relief, including injunctive relief, it could not award compensatory damages, which the common law courts could provide. There was thus a formal need for a representative action that could result in compensatory damages. This was addressed with the fusion of the courts of law and equity in 1873 with the Supreme Court of Judicature Act and Rule 10 of the Rules of Procedure.[17] With this fusion, Parliament widened the scope of the representative action by extending its reach into the common law courts.[18]

Early signs of a new era for representative actions after this fusion were promising. The first decision invoking Rule 10 breathed life into the view that the introduction of the rule was a signal that the courts were becoming sensitive to the exigencies of modern life and the collective problems that

---

[16] Kazanjian (n 11) at 401.

[17] Rule 10 of the Rules of Procedure held: 'Where there are numerous parties having the same interest in one action, one or more of such parties may sue or be sued or may be authorised by the Court to defend in such action on behalf of or for the benefit of all parties so interested', Ontario Law Reform Commission (n 12) at 6.

[18] M.A. Eizenga and E. Davis, 'A History of Class Actions: Modern Lessons from Deep Roots' (2011) 7(1) *Canadian Class Action Review* 9.

arose therein. In *Duke of Bedford v Ellis* (1901), a case involving fruit and vegetable growers and their entitlement to preferential rights at Covent Garden Market, the representative action was approved in spite of relatively strong arguments in favour of the claim being brought forward on individual bases by the respective growers.[19] 'Given a common interest and a common grievance,' Lord Macnaghten observed, 'a representative suit was in order if the relief sought was in its nature beneficial to all whom the plaintiff proposed to represent.'[20] This principle was reaffirmed later that same year in *Taff Vale Railway Co v Amalgamated Society of Railway Servants* (1901), in which the Lords observed obiter that the 'principle is as applicable to new cases as to old, and ought to be applied to the exigencies of modern life as the occasion requires'.[21] It appeared, then, that the representative action was well on its way to taking its place as an important tool for collective claims-making with the support of a judiciary that recognized its progressive and socially responsive character.

The early promise, however, was short lived. In 1910 the English Court of Appeal reversed course on what had been an expansive interpretation of Rule 10 towards a far more restrictive approach in *Markt & Co Ltd v Knight Steamship Co Ltd* (1910).[22] During the Russo-Japanese War of 1904–05, the Russian Navy sank a cargo ship suspected of carrying contraband. The owners of the non-contraband cargo, recognizing that seeking compensation from the Russian government was not a viable strategy, subsequently sued the ship's owners for damages. For the court, the case involved 43 separate and distinct contracts that could have resulted in separate defences on the part of the ship owner, if these were advanced on individual

---

[19] [1901] AC 1 (HL).
[20] ibid at 8.
[21] [1901] AC 426 at 443 (HL).
[22] [1910] 2 KB 1021 (CA) [*Markt*].

bases.[23] This was a main impediment to the case proceeding as a representative action and created a serious restriction for such actions moving forward.

The other major reason why the court rejected the case as a representative action was due to the damages involved. 'Damages are personal only,' stated Lord Justice Fletcher Moulton; 'no representative action can lie where the sole relief sought is damages, because they have to be proved separately in the case of each plaintiff, and therefore the possibility of representation ceases'.[24] In other words, the main benefit and advancement of representative actions that occurred with Parliament's fusion of law and equity – the potential for the progressive development of representative actions involving compensatory damages – was effectively countermanded by the judiciary. This restrictive approach sought, in the words of one commentator echoing language that would later be used against the modern class action, to reinforce the primacy of individual rights and to ensure 'that this unruly child of equity would not corrupt the orderly procedures of the common law'.[25] The decision of the Court of Appeal, and the expressed stance on the perceived individuality of damages, ultimately cast a long shadow over collective claims-making in England and Wales.[26]

More broadly, for Fletcher Moulton LJ, there was another, more fundamental issue at stake in this case: any one of the ship cargo owners could advance a claim and conduct litigation on behalf of all the others, including those who may not have consented to the litigation, with the effect that any decision

---

[23] ibid at 1040.

[24] ibid.

[25] D. Kell, 'Before the High Court – Representative Actions: Continued Evolution or a Classless Society?' (1993) 15 *Sydney Law Review* 528.

[26] This is evident even to the present day. In interviews conducted for this book with civil justice stakeholders, several critics of class actions made explicit references to *Markt* and argued that damages must be treated individually rather than collectively.

would be binding on all members of the class.[27] To be sure, concerns with due process, representation and individual rights are pervasive in the scholarship and debates over representative or class actions, which is one of the reasons why such actions require a strong judiciary that is capable of close supervision so as to prevent abuses of process.[28] That is also why the interests of absent class members have figured prominently in reforms and reviews of established class action regimes, including those in the United States, Canada and Australia.

Perhaps the most far-reaching effect of *Markt*, however, has been the interpretation of the 'same interest' requirement. According to the court, this requirement means that all the members of the group have to demonstrate identical issues of fact and law.[29] This implies that the group not only has to prove the same contract between all its members and the defendant, but also the same defence by the defendant against all members, and the same relief claimed by all members. The extremely strict approach to the 'same interest' requirement has meant that remarkably few cases have been advanced as representative actions since the decision. Although the courts have sought, in various ways, to relax this requirement, including removing the barrier of a single contract and allowing separate defences against group members, its continued strict approach has been one of the reasons cited by scholars in arguing for the need

---

[27] As Fletcher Moulton LJ observed: 'But that which to my mind most strikingly indicates the fundamental error of the suggestion that the circumstances of these cases justify a representative action is that I can conceive no excuse for allowing any one shipper to conduct litigation on behalf of another without his leave, and yet so as to bind him', [1910] 2 KB 1021 (CA).

[28] This includes, notably, the possibility of actions that have arisen out of collusion with the defendant(s).

[29] The Court of Appeal held that the 'same interest' is evident when there is 'a common interest arising, for instance, under a common document; a common grievance; and; a remedy beneficial to all, but not damages', [1901] 2 KB 1021 (CA).

for class action reform.[30] As Rachael Mulheron has observed, to this day there has been a 'judicial shackling of the rule, to the point where it lacks any degree of reasonable utility at all, except in the most limited of cases'.[31]

Collective legal entity

To the extent that one of the main sources of demand for the representative action arose out of the commercial relationships of unincorporated businesspersons – or, more broadly, groups of persons engaged in economic activities – over the course of the 19th century, the growth of the limited liability corporation which offered such businesspersons the benefits of operating as a single legal entity meant that this demand was significantly reduced.[32] This reduced demand by powerful social and economic actors, in conjunction with the judiciary's restrictive approach, went a long way towards slowing the development of the representative action. Just as such actions offered a procedural vehicle, however, for these groups of unincorporated businesspersons to advance their claims and protect their interests prior to the advent of a modern corporate personality, so too did such actions offer groups of workers protection of

---

[30] The under-utilization of the representative action has occurred despite attempts at gradual relaxation or broadening of its scope, including, eg, in *Prudential Assurance Co Ltd v Newman Industries Ltd* [1981] 1 Ch 229, which expanded the scope of claims to include tort and group damages that could be individually claimed by group members, and *EMI Records Ltd v Riley* [1981] 1 WLR 923, which importantly expanded the scope by allowing for recoverable damages in cases where the quantum owed to the class as a whole could be determined.

[31] R. Mulheron, '*Emerald Supplies Ltd v British Airways plc:* A Century Later, the Ghost of *Markt* Lives On' (2009) 8 *Competition Law Journal* 159; see also R. Mulheron, 'A Missed Gem of an Opportunity for the Representative Rule' (2012) 21 *European Business Law Review* 49.

[32] Kazanjian (n 11) at 400.

their legal rights prior to the growth of labour unions that could offer workers such protection.[33]

This is true to the present day. In the absence of labour unions, such a legal vehicle can offer protection of workers' rights. According to the Department for Business, Energy and Industrial Strategy, there has been a steady decline of union density in the United Kingdom since the late 1970s to the latest official rate of 23.5 per cent in 2019.[34] This indicates a significant vulnerability and, by extension, a need for legal protection for a large majority of the workforce. It is a particularly pressing need for workers in the private sector, given the striking public–private divide in union density, with 52.3 per cent of public sector workers belonging to a labour union compared with only 13.3 per cent in the private sector.[35] When one class action scholar observed, in 1973, that '[u]ntil labour unions were statutorily invested with some degree of legal personality, the procedure for groups of workers wishing to unite in the enforcement of their legal rights was, and to some extent still is, the class action',[36] this was an astute observation made during the peak years of union density. In the decades since, with this steady decline, the importance of the class action as a vehicle for worker protection has only increased. This is why the trade union movement in the United Kingdom has repeatedly called on government to introduce class actions to tackle not only unequal pay cases, but also other labour issues such as the national minimum wage and discrimination.

'The reality is that the most vulnerable workers in our society find it very difficult to stand up for themselves, and

---

[33] ibid at 436.

[34] Department for Business, Energy & Industrial Strategy, 'Trade Union Membership, UK 1995–2019: Statistical Bulletin', *National Statistics*, 27 May 2020.

[35] ibid.

[36] Kazanjian (n 11) at 436.

they fear victimisation,' Baroness Clark observed in a debate on the Employment Bill in the Commons Chamber in July 2008. 'There is therefore a strong case for looking at how organisations such as trade unions can take collective class actions when the law is breached.'[37] That class actions are only available in the Competition Appeal Tribunal in England and Wales and representative actions continue to be restricted, most notably by a strict view of the 'same interest' criterion, suggests that entire areas of social and economic life, not least those involving labour (especially non-unionized labour), are left without adequate legal means for the enforcement of collective interests.

The story told so far has been one of judicial innovation, and restriction, with the fusion of law and equity signalling that Parliament had also played its part.[38] These developments were motivated in large part by what can be labelled as 'internal' concerns in the administration of justice; that is, concerns over the clogging of courts, multiple duplicative cases and the need to ensure consistency in decisions across these cases. This contrasts with what can be labelled as 'external' concerns having to do with opening up the courts to those who would not have otherwise been able to pursue their claims; concerns that would arise more prominently over the course of the 20th century with changing social and political attitudes and the burgeoning 'access to justice' movement. There is perhaps no jurisdiction that took on board these considerations more quickly than the United States.

---

[37] HL Deb (14 July 2008) vol. 479, available at https://hansard.parliament.uk/ Commons/2008-07-14/debates/0807141000002/EmploymentBill(Lor ds)?highlight=%22class%20actions%22#contribution-08071416000135.

[38] This obviously does not imply that the fusion of law and equity was motivated by concerns to address the earlier-mentioned gap for representative actions, but only that this was, if not an explicit motivation, a welcome by-product of this fusion.

United States of America

The development of the representative action in the United States can be rooted to the adoption of the rule in the common law in 1820 in *West v Randall*, followed by Equity Rule 48 becoming the first such rule in the federal courts in 1833.[39] Importantly, however, Equity Rule 48 did not bind absent members. This was addressed by the US Supreme Court in 1843, but it was not until 1912 that the rule was amended, now called Equity Rule 38, to expressly hold that all such absent members could be so bound.[40] This rule obtained until the first appearance of Rule 23 of the United States Federal Rules of Civil Procedure, which was adopted in 1938.[41] This newly formulated Rule 23, while beneficial insofar as it extended the scope of such actions to include both legal and equitable remedies, suffered from a deficient classification system (between so-called true, hybrid and spurious class actions) that demanded further reform. By the late 1940s, the rule had come to be viewed as unsatisfactory, cumbersome and, in the words of one commentator, 'euphonious, if mystic'.[42]

---

[39] Eizanga and Davis (n 18) at 9; see also D. Hensler, N. Pace, B. Dombey-Moore, E. Giddens, J. Gross and E. Moller, *Class Action Dilemmas: Pursuing Public Goals for Private Gain* (Santa Monica, CA: Rand, 2001) at 10–11. For a good overview, see D. Marcus, 'The History of the Modern Class Action, Part I: Sturm und Drang, 1953–1980' (2013) 90(3) *Washington University Law Review* 1–63, and D. Marcus, 'The History of the Modern Class Action, Part II: Litigation and Legitimacy, 1981–1994', *Arizona Legal Studies: Discussion Paper No. 17-17* (2017) at 1–79.

[40] Equity Rule 38 provided that 'When the question is one of common or general interest to many persons constituting a class so numerous as to make it impracticable to bring them all before the court, one or more may sue or defend for the whole', Hensler et al (n 39) at 11.

[41] Eizenga and Davis (n 18) at 10; Ontario Law Reform Commission (n 12) at 8.

[42] *Dickinson v Burnham*, 197 F.2d 973, 978 (2d Cir. 1952); *Sys. Fed'n No. 91 v Reed*, 180 F.2d 991, 996 (6th Cir. 1950); *Martinez v Maverick Cnty. Water Control and Improvement Dist.*, 219 F.2d 666 (5th Cir. 1955); *Pentland v. Dravo Corporation*, 152 F.2d 851 (3d Cir. 1945) at 852.

During this period, there was a growing recognition of the role that litigation can play in a healthy functioning democracy. Whereas historically jurists tended to hold 'a deeply entrenched English attitude that litigation itself was a socially disruptive evil',[43] this normative stance was progressively challenged in the 20th century, notably in the United States during the class action reform process. As Harry Kalven and Maurice Rosenfeld famously argued in 1941, the class action needed to be reformed to actively encourage private lawyers as public-oriented citizens, later termed 'private attorneys general', to deploy it as a policy instrument in a broader regulatory effort.[44] As we will see in Chapter Three, this vision of the class action as a political tool that serves to empower vulnerable people against powerful adversaries has come under scrutiny from both partisans and legal scholars who view the modern class action in a more limited lens. For now, it suffices to note that despite their prescient analysis of the role that class actions could, and in some ways eventually would, play as a form of private enforcement, the liberal reformers and drafters of the Federal Rules of Civil Procedure had more modest ambitions.

Calls for reform of the original Rule 23 started in earnest in 1948 and continued into the 1950s – efforts that bore no fruit until the 1960s, when the Supreme Court reinstated the Advisory Committee and efforts began anew. To underscore the importance of the historical context in which the modern class action arose, the only substantive consideration that was raised during the deliberations of the Advisory Committee was the issue of desegregation of schools for African American students and the necessity of developing a legal vehicle that could adequately address civil rights.[45] John

---

[43] Ontario Law Reform Commission (n 12) at 717.

[44] H. Kalven and M. Rosenfield, 'The Contemporary Function of the Class Action Suit' (1941) 8 *University of Chicago Law Review* 684.

[45] John P. Frank, Response to 1996 Circulation of Proposed Rule 23 on Class Actions, in 2 *Working Papers of the Advisory Committee on Civil Rules*

P. Frank, a member of the Committee, noted plainly: 'If there was a single, undoubted goal of the committee, the energizing force which motivated the whole rule, it was the firm determination to create a class action system which could deal with civil rights and, explicitly, segregation.'[46] The modern class action was thus offered as an answer to the question of how to avoid numerous duplicative cases seeking integration and redress for discrimination for African-Americans, particularly in the American South.[47]

Even at the outset of its creation, however, some of the concerns about class actions that are common today were voiced. Frank himself raised concerns about the prospect of improper conduct by lawyers who may be tempted to act in ways contrary to the interests of their clients through early settlements that undervalued the claims of the class.[48] The finality of *res judicata* – the principle that once a matter has been adjudicated by a competent court then it may not be pursued any further by the parties and thus global peace will be ensured – was also cause for concern. 'It is practical child's play for some business,' Frank noted, 'which wishes to escape the consequences of its acts to have the suit brought by a dummy who purports to represent a class, let him lose it, and thus escape responsibility'.[49] Although this has largely proven

---

on *Proposed Amendments to Civil Rule 23* at 262, 266, available at www.fjc.gov.

[46] ibid.

[47] G. Calabresi, 'Class Actions in the US Experience: The Legal Perspective' in J.G. Backhaus, A. Cassone and G.B. Ramello (eds), *The Law and Economics of Class Actions in Europe: Lessons from America* (Cheltenham: Edward Elgar, 2012) at 13.

[48] ibid.

[49] Letter from John Frank to Benjamin Kaplan, at 2 (Jan. 21, 1963), in Records of the U.S. Judicial Conference, microformed on CIS No. CI-6312–20 (Cong. Info. Serv.); D. Marcus, 'The History of the Modern Class Action, Part I: Sturm und Drang, 1953–1980' (2013) 90(3) *Washington University Law Review* 1–63.

to be an unfounded fear, it was considered serious enough that the Advisory Committee required in the new law that all settlements and fees must be approved by a judge in order to prevent any such 'sweetheart deals'. Today, the idea that the class action could somehow be considered a beneficial development for corporations will strike commentators as rather odd. As one outspoken American conservative scholar has observed, looking back at these modern origins, 'letting the new class action become law was no doubt the biggest mistake corporate America has ever made with regard to our system of civil justice'.[50] If current lobbying efforts are any indication, this is a mistake that corporate interests have sought not to repeat in other jurisdictions that have debated the adoption of class actions.

A vital development with 1966's Rule 23 was the introduction of a certification stage, a pre-trial stage in which the plaintiffs have to demonstrate that they meet certain stipulated criteria in order for their claim to be certified as a class action. In the decades since, certification has often proved to be a major battleground between the parties, and once a class action is certified as such it often results in a negotiated settlement. By extension, of course, in class action reforms in the United States and elsewhere, the criteria to be determined at certification have also been a battleground, with critics seeking to restrict or tighten these criteria, often introducing new requirements that seek to make certification more difficult for prospective claimants, with proponents advocating in the opposite direction. In 1966 the new Rule 23(a) held that a claim could be certified if it met the four key criteria of (1) numerosity, which simply means that there are enough people involved in the claim to make proceeding as a class action worthwhile; (2) commonality, which simply means that there is sufficient

---

[50] B.T. Fitzpatrick, *The Conservative Case for Class Actions* (Chicago, IL: University of Chicago Press, 2019) at 11.

common issues of law and fact; (3) typicality, which refers to the understanding that the claims (or defences) of the representative should be typical of the claims (or defences) of the class; and (4) adequacy of representative, which is a determination on the ability of the representative to fairly and adequately protect the interests of the class, recalling the aforementioned concern raised in *Markt*.[51] In addition, any action also has to satisfy Rule 23(b), which sets out three categories of class actions, including the important third category which allows for damages as a remedy and sets out the requirement that the common issues need to 'predominate' over the individual issues, as well as a 'superiority' requirement, which holds that the class action needs to be superior to other available methods of adjudication.

In contrast to later reform processes, both in the United States and elsewhere, the reform of Rule 23 did not elicit much lobbying from partisans, whether from corporations and their allies or from traditional proponents such as labour unions, human rights groups, environmentalists or consumer protection organizations. It was a closed-door affair undertaken without much publicity or protest, by a group of 15–16 jurists, appointed by the Chief Justice of the Supreme Court, gathering in the conference room of Covington & Burling, the law firm where the Chair of the Committee, Dean Acheson,

---

[51] Rule 23(a) of the Federal Rules of Civil Procedure holds as follows:

  (a) Prerequisites. One or more members of a class may sue or be sued as representative parties on behalf of all members only if:

  (1) the class is so numerous that joinder of all members is impracticable;

  (2) there are questions of law or fact common to the class;

  (3) the claims or defenses of the representative parties are typical of the claims or defenses of the class; and

  (4) the representative parties will fairly and adequately protect the interests of the class.

was a senior partner.[52] As some committee members have acknowledged in hindsight, the group set about the reforms without fully appreciating the controversial behemoth that the class action would eventually become.[53] 'The massive growth of class actions was not intended,' Arthur Miller, a committee member has observed; this growth 'was a product of the unforeseen social forces and doctrinal shifts that went well beyond civil rights'.[54]

For the members of the Advisory Committee, the modern class action was originally intended to have a much more limited application. The wide range of cases that make the class action such an important procedure today in the promotion of collective access to justice was viewed in the early 1960s as not suitable for the vehicle.[55] For the Advisory Committee, even mass torts or product liability cases, which are today viewed as prototypical cases, were not considered appropriate.[56]

It was not long before this initial constrained view came under question. As early as 1972, the Judicial Conference of the United States observed that class actions were proliferating

---

[52] A. Miller and S. Issacharoff, 'Rule 23 @ 50: The 50th Anniversary of Rule 23: An Oral History of Rule 23', Center on Civil Justice, New York University School of Law, 3 December 2016.

[53] See, eg, B.T. Fitzpatrick, *The Conservative Case for Class Actions* (Chicago, IL: University of Chicago Press, 2019) at 9–12.

[54] Miller and Issacharoff (n 52) at 8.

[55] As committee member Arthur Miller has observed:

> When drafted, it had a modest dimension. There was a sense that in application it would have a limited application. It has proven to have a dimension many times the size of anything conceived of by the people in that room. The best proceduralists in the United States were on that Committee. We had every significant academic proceduralist and some of the best district judges.

ibid at 8.

[56] J. Resnik, 'From "Cases" to "Litigation"' (1991) 54 *Law and Contemporary Problems* 9–11.

at rapid speed and commissioned a study to examine the extent of their application. It found that about 3,148 class actions were pending in the federal court, with 43.5 per cent of these (1,369 actions) being civil rights class actions, which of course was not wholly unexpected given its original purpose; but that 20 per cent of these pending actions related to securities and commodities, and 10 per cent were anti-trust actions, came as something of a surprise.[57] It reflected the growing recognition of the economic incentives involved in such mass actions by entrepreneurial lawyers. This would become one of the main points of debate as class actions grew in prominence in subsequent decades, not only in the United States, but also in states considering adopting the procedure. The role of entrepreneurialism, and the abuses that could stem from entrepreneurial litigation, raised concerns about the extent to which class actions were responsible for commodifying law enforcement.[58]

If there were any doubts about their wide applicability in the late 1960s, these were put to rest in the 1970s and 1980s with a series of Supreme Court decisions in favour of class actions that broadened their appeal. This was the period where the mass torts class action, originally a type of action that was explicitly cited as something unsuitable for the procedure, became a widespread phenomenon, as well as litigation involving asbestos, product liability, labour disputes and employment civil rights cases involving discrimination based on disability, sex, age and race – in addition to the aforementioned suits

---

[57] J. Coffee, *Entrepreneurial Litigation: Its Rise, Fall, and Future* (Cambridge, MA: Harvard University Press, 2015) at 63.

[58] One of the curious twists in class action history is that such concerns have typically been raised by corporate critics of class actions, such as the US Chamber of Commerce, who have generally not been opposed to entrepreneurialism, marketization, or commodification in other areas of social and economic life, as opposed to traditional progressive critics of such economic forces, who have historically been among the most ardent advocates for class actions.

relating to shareholders, securities and commodities, and antitrust claims.[59]

Since that time, however, ongoing retrenchment efforts have sought to restrict their purview in various ways, notably with the passage of the somewhat ironically named Class Actions Fairness Act of 2005, introduced by Congressman Sensenbrenner, the Republican head of the House Judiciary Committee.[60] Among its notable impacts, CAFA removed large-scale class actions out of state courts and into federal courts; the former being far more hospitable to class actions than the latter.

Such retrenchment has not been limited to legislative reforms as the judiciary has also taken an active role. If the 'invention and development of the class action was the dominant judicial innovation of the late twentieth century', John Coffee has observed, then 'its dismantling appears to be the major procedural project of the conservative majority of the contemporary Supreme Court in the twenty-first century'.[61] In the past two decades, the court has successfully restricted class actions across a wide range of areas, including employment discrimination and mass torts. In so doing, the court has partly neutralized the economic enablers that have been a driving force for class actions. This includes capping fees for class lawyers and restricting punitive damages via constitutional limits.[62] Perhaps most problematically, the court has legitimated the use of mandatory arbitration clauses in standard form contracts, which form an 'insurmountable barrier to litigation in court'[63] and serve to individualize otherwise collective justiciable problems and take these out of the public courts and into private dispute resolution fora. The mobilization of mandatory arbitration

---

[59] Calabresi (n 47) at 15–16.

[60] Class Action Fairness Act of 2005, Pub. L. No. 109-2, 119 Stat. 4.

[61] Coffee (n 57) at 2.

[62] ibid.

[63] ibid. This recalls the broader criticisms raised about the ADR movement.

clauses, and clauses that explicitly prevent individuals from joining class actions, has been an effective method used by potential defendants in preventing vulnerable persons from accessing justice in court.

As one Democratic Congressman noted, CAFA is 'the final payback to the tobacco industry, to the asbestos industry, to the oil industry, to the chemical industry at the expense of ordinary families who need to be able to go to court to protect their loved ones'.[64] Democratic congresswoman Nancy Pelosi also observed that when people are 'injured or even killed by Vioxx or Celebrex or discriminated against by Wal-Mart, they may never get their day in court'.[65] In contrast to the widespread perception of the United States being the dominant state for class actions globally, the current civil justice landscape suggests that the heyday of the American class action is in the past.

Canada

The restrictive approach of *Markt* in the English courts had a long-lasting effect on the development of representative actions in Canada. Only a slight change was notable in the statutory regimes, when Ontario modified Rule 10 in 1980 into Rule 75 in the Ontario *Rules of Practice*.[66] The slow development of representative actions was similarly evident in the judiciary, where courts found 'little guidance' in Rule 75, which resulted

---

[64] The Association of Trial Lawyers of America also observed that CAFA was 'a shameful attack on Americans' legal rights'. William Branigin, 'Congress today handed Presiden …', *The Washington Post*, February 17, 2005, available at https://www.washingtonpost.com/archive/business/technology/2005/02/17/congress-today-handed-presiden/9d6047c9-9628-4778-9e12-d76e0e8c197d/.

[65] ibid.

[66] The new Rule 75 held, quite similarly to the previous Rule 10: 'Where there are numerous persons having the same interest, one or more may sue or be sued or may be authorized by the court to defend on behalf of, or for the benefit of, all.' *Revised Regulations of Ontario* 1980, Reg 540.

in a 'conservative and at times confusing approach'[67] that can be 'more seriously described as illogical'.[68] It would be left to the legislature to introduce any changes to the restrictive landscape.[69] Although Quebec introduced class action legislation in 1978, as the only civil law regime in an otherwise common law state, its impact on the rest of Canada was minimal.[70] In Ontario, starting in 1976, the Ontario Law Reform Commission began a reform process in earnest, ultimately publishing, in 1982, the influential *Report on Class Actions* ('OLRC Report').

The OLRC Report laid out the three main objectives of class actions that provincial legislatures and courts, including the Supreme Court, would eventually identify: access to justice, judicial economy, and behaviour modification. The first objective of promoting access to justice for collectives and groups of similarly situated individuals is self-evident. The second objective of judicial economy refers to what this author has previously described as 'internal concerns' in the

---

[67] Eizenga and Davis (n 18) at 14.

[68] ibid. As one commentator noted at the time:

> The law respecting class actions and, in particular, the interpretation of Rule 75 and its counterparts elsewhere, has been characterized by uncertainty and, more importantly, has been distinguished by a reliance on formalistic and non-functional categorizations to differentiate actions appropriately brought as class actions from those that are not. The result has been a body of case law that can fairly be regarded as conservative, and more seriously described as illogical.

> L.M. Fox, 'Naken v General Motors of Canada Ltd.: Class Actions Deferred' (1984) 6 *Supreme Court Law Review* 336.

[69] The Supreme Court of Canada was in a position to modify this approach and restore the more progressive approach of the English courts prior to *Markt* in *Naken v General Motors of Canada* [1983] 1 SCR 72.

[70] An Act Respecting the Class Action, SQ 1978, c 8. It came into force on 19 January 1979.

administration of justice, namely, the benefits of preserving scarce judicial resources by aggregating similar claims into a single vehicle. The third objective of behaviour modification refers to the role of class actions as policy instruments in a private enforcement regime and their potential role in deterring misconduct by similarly situated wrongdoers. In the decades since the report's publication, the first two objectives have come to be seen as primary goals of class action legislation, whereas the third objective has been viewed as a secondary goal.

The reasoning that the OLRC Report set out for this reform process is worth considering. It arose as a response to the recognition that the individualism that has distinguished the paradigm of the common law does not reflect the types of justiciable problems with which people are today confronted.[71] 'In the past,' the OLRC Report observes at its very outset, 'we generally have accepted as fair and reasonable the often heavy burden of ultimately vindicating our rights by the commencement of individual legal proceedings.'[72] And yet '[i]ndividualistic notions

---

[71] By prefacing the Report with this observation, the authors recognize that the individualism they are describing is not solely a feature of the common law jurisprudence, but has much deeper roots socially, philosophically and culturally:

> Individualism, the belief in the free and independent action of individuals, is a concept that has deep roots in Western society. While by no means universally or unequivocally adopted by all persons and in all circumstances, the notion that one can, and indeed must, be the architect of one's own destiny is reflected in the traditional manner in which people have related to the social, economic, political, and other institutions in our society.

Ontario Law Reform Commission (n 12) at 2–3. Although this perspective discounts, in many ways, the collectivism that has been a distinguished feature of so-called 'Western' society, it does well to identify, if only in a roundabout way, one of the main philosophical sticking points for critics of representative or class actions.

[72] ibid at 3.

of our capacity to assert and protect our legal rights by acting alone were, of course, never entirely in accordance with the often harsh facts'.[73] In the face of radically changing social and economic conditions, the individualistic 'perspective of our place in society is today somewhat outdated – an anachronism often more a reflection of nostalgia than reality'.[74] Recalling the similar observation of Cappelletti and Garth in the *Florence Project*, the OLRC Report thus set out its raison d'être: given the social and economic order in which we live, 'dramatic changes in production, promotion, and consumption have given rise to what may be called "mass wrongs" – that is, injury or damage to many persons caused by the same or very similar sets of circumstances'.[75] The OLRC Report ultimately observed that the ways in which 'other existing procedural alternatives to protect legal rights where mass wrongs are involved', which included the traditional representative action, as well as joinder, consolidation, and test cases, 'do not fill the present legal vacuum' and thus advocated for class action legislation to address these gaps.[76] Given that this civil landscape is similar to that which can be found in other states, the OLRC Report has proven to be influential beyond Canada's borders, being cited by numerous reform processes, including in England and Wales.

Taking on board many of its recommendations, the Ontario legislature introduced, after a circuitous political journey, its class action legislation in 1992.[77] It was only with the passage of the Class Proceedings Act that the proverbial tide turned in Canada, as successive common law provinces introduced their own respective legislation in turn. British Columbia[78] adopted

---

[73] ibid.

[74] ibid.

[75] ibid.

[76] ibid at 4.

[77] Class Proceedings Act, SO 1992, c 6. It came into force on 1 January 1993.

[78] First enacted as SBC 1995, c 21, followed by the Class Proceedings Act, RSBC 1996, c 50.

its class action legislation in 1995, followed by Saskatchewan[79] and Newfoundland[80] in 2002, Manitoba[81] in 2003, and Alberta[82] in 2004. New Brunswick[83] and Nova Scotia[84] also followed suit in 2006 and 2007, respectively.

In Ontario, the major regime in Canada by volume, the CPA outlines the criteria to be used by courts at certification to determine whether or not a proceeding can advance as a class action. These five criteria hold that there must be (1) a cause of action, (2) an identifiable class of two or more persons, (3) common issues raised by the class, (4) the class action must be a preferable procedure, and (5) there must be a viable representative plaintiff.[85] In the regime so far, the criteria of (2) an identifiable class and (5) a representative plaintiff have been relatively straightforward to satisfy, whereas the other three criteria have proven to be more difficult. This is borne out by statistical data from the Law Commission of Ontario's Final

---

[79] Class Actions Act, SS 2001, c C-12.01.

[80] Class Actions Act, SNL 2001, c C-18.1.

[81] Class Proceedings Act, CCSM, c C130.

[82] Class Proceedings Act, SA 2003, c C-16.5.

[83] Class Proceedings Act, SNB 2006, c C-5.15.

[84] Class Proceedings Act, SNS 2007, c 28.

[85] As per the CPA, s 5(1), the Court shall certify a class proceeding if:

> (a) the pleadings or the notice of application discloses a cause of action;
> (b) there is an identifiable class of two or more persons that would be represented by the representative plaintiff or defendant;
> (c) the claims or defences of the class members raise common issues;
> (d) a class proceeding would be the preferable procedure for the resolution of the common issues; and
> (e) there is a representative plaintiff or defendant who,
>> (i) would fairly and adequately represent the interests of the class,
>> (ii) has produced a plan for the proceeding that sets out a workable method of advancing the proceeding on behalf of the class and of notifying class members of the proceeding, and
>> (iii) does not have, on the common issues for the class, an interest in conflict with the interests of the other class members.

Report (2019), which shows that the two most frequently cited grounds for dismissal at certification are the (3) commonality and (4) preferability criteria at 47 per cent and 46 per cent respectively, with the (1) cause of action criterion cited at a rate of 27 per cent and the remaining two criteria of (2) an identifiable class and (5) a viable representative plaintiff cited at a rate of 19 per cent and 11 per cent each.

At the outset, as with most such legislation, there was a fair amount of caution from justice stakeholders, from prospective plaintiff class action firms and from the judiciary. It was only with a trilogy of decisions by the Supreme Court in the early 2000s that breathed new life into the vehicle that the respective provincial regimes blossomed. The first of these cases was *Western Canadian Shopping Centres v Dutton* (2001) where the Supreme Court took the significant step of recognizing that class actions were of such public importance that they warranted adoption into the common law.[86] With the exception of Prince Edward Island, every province has since introduced class action legislation. As Chief Justice Beverley McLachlin confirmed at the time, underscoring the access to justice benefits of the vehicle: 'Without class actions, the doors of justice remain closed to some plaintiffs, however strong their legal claims.'[87]

---

[86] SCJ 63, 2 SCR 534.

[87] ibid at 28. McLachlin J also elaborated on the three main objectives of class actions, echoing the OLRC Report and worth quoting in full:

> Class actions offer three important advantages over a multiplicity of individual suits. First, by aggregating similar individual suits, class actions serve judicial economy by avoiding unnecessary duplication in fact-finding and legal analysis. The efficiencies thus generated free judicial resources that can be directed at resolving other conflicts, and can also reduce the costs of litigation both for plaintiffs (who can share litigation costs) and for defendants (who need to litigate the disputed issue only once, rather than numerous times).

In the second of this trilogy, *Hollick v Toronto (City)* (2001), the Supreme Court championed a flexible and progressive approach to certification. To the extent that certification is the major battleground for prospective class actions, the so-called 'Hollick approach' was a boon to claimants seeking collective access to justice. Finally, in the third case, *Rumley v British Columbia* (2001), the Supreme Court moved beyond the prevailing economistic rationale for class actions. The case involved the institutional abuse of blind and deaf children and gave rise to the growing recognition that class actions could go a long way in overcoming the social and psychological barriers that groups may face in accessing justice.[88] In the years since this trilogy, class actions in Canada's provincial regimes have flourished.[89]

Second, by allowing fixed litigation costs to be divided over a large number of plaintiffs, class actions improve access to justice by making economical the prosecution of claims that would otherwise be too costly to prosecute individually. Without class actions, the doors of justice remain closed to some plaintiffs, however strong their legal claims. Sharing costs ensures that injuries are not left unremedied.

Third, class actions serve efficiency and justice by ensuring that actual and potential wrongdoers do not ignore their obligations to the public. Without class actions, those who cause widespread but individually minimal harm might not take into account the full costs of their conduct, because for any one plaintiff the expense of bringing suit would far exceed the likely recovery. Cost-sharing decreases the expense of pursuing legal recourse and accordingly deters potential defendants who might otherwise assume minor wrongs would not result in litigation.

[88] This was already recognized in the OLRC Report.

[89] A recent overview, undertaken by the Law Commission of Ontario, into the first 25 years of Ontario's regime, offered a series of recommendations for improving the functioning of class actions in that province with respect to the Class Proceedings Act's three policy objectives of improving access to justice, ensuring judicial economy and promoting behaviour modification (re: the deterrence function). See Law Commission of

In line with the history of eliciting adverse reforms, there have been noticeable efforts at retrenchment in Canada, perhaps most notably the introduction of Bill 161, the Smarter and Stronger Justice Act, 2020, by the Conservative government of Doug Ford in Ontario. In addition to more sweeping and severe reforms to legal aid provisioning in the province, this legislation takes aim at class actions by introducing a restrictive criterion at certification that the common issues of law and fact need to predominate over the individual issues, as well as a strict superiority criterion that holds that the class action needs to be superior to all other available methods of adjudication. These mandatory provisions – predominance and superiority – serve to strengthen the hand of defendants at certification. As expected, the proposed legislation has come under intense scrutiny by scholars and access to justice advocates. In a public reply, the Law Commission of Ontario observed that the proposed amendments will 'increase costs, lengthen delays, and undermine access to justice and judicial efficiency'.[90] The Law Commission of Ontario also observed that a range of important actions in the past would not have been certified if the proposed criteria were retroactively applied, including the Residential Schools action involving the abuse of Indigenous children, as well as cases involving environmental claims, product and medical liability, and claims against the government.[91]

Ontario, *Class Actions: Objectives, Experiences and Reforms – Final Report* (Toronto: July 2019).

[90] Law Commission of Ontario, 'Re: Class Proceedings Amendments, Bill 161, the *Smarter and Stronger Justice Act*' (Law Commission of Ontario, 22 January 2020), available at https://www.lco-cdo.org/wp-content/uploads/2020/01/LCO-Letter-re-Bill-161-Class-Actions-Final-Jan-22–2020.pdf.

[91] ibid.

Australia

When it comes to class actions in their modern incarnation, the United States can be viewed as a First Generation regime, in terms of its maturity and historical development, with Canada being a regime of the Second Generation.[92] The only other regime in this latter generation is Australia. In a development similar to that in Canada, the established rules governing representative actions in Australia were deemed to be inadequate by the latter decades of the 20th century, leading to several state-funded law reform bodies advocating for the adoption of modern class actions. Notably, in 1988, the Law Reform Commission tabled a report in the federal Parliament that eventually led to the current Australian federal opt-out class action regime, which came into force in 1992.[93] In addition to this new class action regime of Part IVA of the Federal Court Act, another regime was introduced in Victoria eight years later in 2000. In recent years, two other states have introduced class action legislation – Queensland and New South Wales – with other states like Tasmania and Western Australia also taking steps to introduce such legislation.[94] Much like Victoria, both these pieces of state legislation are based on (and nearly identical to) the federal legislation. The majority of class actions in Australia, however, continue to be advanced in the federal court.

In the parliamentary debates over the bill in 1991, the well-established objective of the federal class action was identified as being, first and foremost, the standard economic rationale

---

[92] This metaphor is first developed by leading class action scholar Rachael Mulheron. See, eg, her recent book, *Class Actions and Government* (Cambridge: Cambridge University Press, 2020) at 83.

[93] Law Reform Commission, *Grouped Proceedings in the Federal Court*, Report No. 46 (1988).

[94] Civil Proceedings Act 2011 (QLD), Pt 13A; Civil Procedure Act 2005 (NSW), Pt 10.

for the procedure from an access to justice perspective, which was echoed in Canada and the United States: in order to 'provide a real remedy where, although many people are affected and the total amount at issue is significant, each person's loss is small and not economically viable to recover in individual actions'.[95] As such, a class action procedure will 'give access to the courts to those in the community who have been effectively denied justice because of the high cost of taking action'.[96] This economic rationale will be further explored in Chapter Four.

The second reason offered related to the efficiencies of the procedure. It observed that class actions can improve judicial efficiency in cases 'where the damages sought by each claimant are large enough to justify individual actions and a large number of persons wish to sue the respondent'.[97] Simply put, even in cases where individuals would otherwise have sought damages in court, the class action is desirable to the extent that it allows groups of such individuals 'to obtain redress and do so more cheaply and efficiently than would be the case with individual actions'.[98] According to both reasons, then, the access to justice benefits that would follow from introducing the class action warranted reform.

In addition to the chief objective of promoting access to justice for groups, the Law Reform Commission also observed that class actions have a regulatory function. This refers to the deterrence function, alternatively known as the

---

[95] Commonwealth, *Parliamentary Debates*, House of Representatives, 14 November 1991, 3174 (Michael Duffy, Attorney-General). See also B. Murphy and C. Cameron, 'Access to Justice and the Evolution of Class Action Litigation in Australia' (2006) 30 *Melbourne University Law Review* 402.

[96] ibid.

[97] ibid. Whereas the first reason offered was based on the access to justice benefits for negative value claims, this second reason is based on such benefits for claims with a positive value.

[98] ibid.

policy objective of behaviour modification in the Canadian context. For the Law Reform Commission, the one can lead to the other. In other words, introducing a procedure like class actions that allows 'people to have increased access to legal remedies in court proceedings could render the substantive law more enforceable and thus encourage a greater degree of compliance'.[99] This is an important point that speaks to the need for available procedures that allow for private enforcement. 'Respect for the law,' the Law Reform Commission emphasizes, 'should be enhanced if access to remedies is facilitated.'[100]

Interestingly, the state and federal regimes in Australia do not require certification. In the view of the Law Reform Commission in 1988 – whose report was influential in the establishment of the Federal regime and, by extension, the state regimes – there was no need for a certification stage as this was believed to be an unnecessary step that would only serve to increase cost and delay.[101] There is, however, a threshold test that is conducted, with the requirement that a proposed action must involve (1) at least seven persons against the same person, (2) the claims must arise out of the same, similar or related circumstances, and (3) they must give rise to substantial common issues of fact or law. These are not difficult threshold requirements to meet and courts have taken a liberal and generous approach in conducting the test. Courts may, of course, determine that it is no longer in the interests of justice

---

[99] Law Reform Commission (n 93) at 33.

[100] ibid.

[101] Australian Law Reform Commission Report Grouped Proceedings in the Federal Court No. 46 (1988). There has, however, been some criticism on this point that without certification there has been increased and unnecessarily protracted interlocutory disputes which would conceivably have been avoided if a certification stage had been implemented. See, eg, D. Grave, K. Adams and J. Betts, *Class Actions in Australia*, 2nd edition (Pyrmont, NSW: Thomson Reuters, 2012) at 131.

for a proceeding to continue. Among the notable differences between Australian class actions and those in the United States (and now Ontario) is that there is no predominance requirement where the common issues need to 'predominate' over the individual issues.

One final point warrants a brief mention: as is the case in the United States and Canada, and indeed in most regimes around the world, class actions in Australia are trans-substantive or generic procedures. They apply across the breadth of substantive law. This would not need to be remarked upon as it is normally self-evident that procedure is trans-substantive, but this appears to be a matter of debate, as we will see with developments in England and Wales where the adoption of class action legislation has departed from this long-standing practice.

Conclusion

The First and Second Generation regimes discussed thus far enacted reforms to introduce the modern class action in response to the limitations and inadequacies of the traditional representative action. Notable among these was the lack of protection of the rights and interests of groups of people and the insufficient promotion of collective access to justice. Enacting such reforms on similar bases in England and Wales, by extension, may seem like a straightforward endeavour, given that the conditions that gave rise to such reforms in the First and Second Generation regimes are similarly present in England and Wales. Yet the reform process in this jurisdiction has proven to be rather more challenging, and has been animated, to varying degrees, by fears of the abuses (whether real or imagined) of US-style class actions, social litigiousness, increased adversarial legalism, and a lack of political will, as discussed in the next chapter.

THREE

Uncovering the Politics of Class Actions

As we have noted already, debates over the modern class action have historically been divided along ideological lines, with conservative forces and corporate lobbies, such as the US Chamber of Commerce (and its advocacy body, the Institute for Legal Reform) and the European Justice Forum, seeking to restrict their expansion and delimit their purview, and progressive forces seeking to introduce and expand their scope.[1] This debate is

---

[1] One notable exception to this bifurcation has been a novel argument from a conservative standpoint in favour of class actions made by Brian Fitzpatrick, who plainly observes that 'the reason why I say I believe conservatives turned their back on private enforcement to begin with: class actions are used to enforce laws we don't like'. He goes on to note that 'many conservative scholars do not believe that we should saddle business with minimum wage, overtime, employment discrimination, and employment benefit laws' and the way forward was to attack the trans-substantivity of procedural rules so that conservatives can 'pick and choose' where class actions are available and where they are not. This perspective views the privatization of regulatory enforcement (through vehicles such as class actions) as a positive development to the extent that this could signal reduction in public enforcement and smaller government, thereby allowing market forces to dictate enforcement priorities while also encouraging

both instrumental and ideological in character. It should not come as much of a surprise, then, to discover the extent to which class action discourse and reforms have been animated by such partisanship. As numerous scholars have observed over the years, the strategies of the conservative legal movement have served to distort the law and perpetuate misconceptions that have negatively impacted the capacities of vulnerable people to access justice.[2] This chapter explores the politics of the procedure and analyses the ways in which various interest groups have sought to influence, with varying degrees of success, the development of regimes and their public perception, and offers a closer look at recent developments in England and Wales.

Setting the stage

The partisanship and ideological divide that is evident in debates over class actions is, according to Martin Redish, a result of

---

people to help themselves and take individual responsibility, according to libertarian principles. B.T. Fitzpatrick, *The Conservative Case for Class Actions* (Chicago, IL: University of Chicago Press, 2019) at 29–66, 114–15.

[2] Such outputs include (from the conservative legal movement), M. Boot, *Out of Order: Arrogance, Corruption, and Incompetence on the Bench* (New York, NY: Basic Books, 1998); C.J. Sykes, *A Nation of Victims: The Decay of the American Character* (New York, NY: St. Martin's Press, 1992); W. Olson, *The Excuse Factory: How Employment Law is Paralyzing the American Workplace* (New York, NY: Martin Kessler Books, 1997); P.M. Garry, *A Nation of Adversaries: How the Litigation Explosion is Reshaping America* (New York, NY: Plenum Press, 1997); W. Olson, *The Litigation Explosion* (New York, NY: Truman Talley, 1991). For critical scholarship on this movement, see, eg, W. Haltom and M. McCann, *Distorting the Law: Politics, Media, and the Litigation Crisis* (Chicago, IL: University of Chicago Press, 2004); S. Staszak, *No Day In Court: Access to Justice and the Politics of Judicial Retrenchment* (Oxford: Oxford University Press, 2015); S.M. Teles, *The Rise of the Conservative Legal Movement: The Battle for Control of the Law* (Princeton, NJ: Princeton University Press, 2008); S. Staszak, 'Institutions, Rulemaking, and the Politics of Judicial Retrenchment' (2010) 24(2) *Studies in American Political Development* 168–89.

'litigation socialism', which refers to the purported aims of class actions 'to redistribute wealth from large concentrations of economic power' to vulnerable people and communities.[3] This redistributive facet is decried by critics who challenge the premises of redistributive justice at an ideological level, as well as the legitimacy of achieving redistributive justice through private legal action. That is why, as Redish observes, the class action debate has 'broken down along ideological lines: the political left has reflexively favoured the device and the political right has reflexively opposed it'.[4]

The very function of class actions as forms of collective claims-making has also come under scrutiny.[5] For critics, the class action is an 'island of collectivism in a sea of individualised dispute resolution', which serves as a 'rejection of liberal process-based individualism'.[6] This rejection of liberal individualism is the 'elephant in the room' to the extent that the 'inherent collectivism' of class actions creates a tension with legal systems premised on liberal principles of individual autonomy and identity. Others have added that class actions 'loom as a subversive element' and from 'the perspective of the common law tradition of individual justice, class actions are a necessary evil, but an evil nonetheless'.[7]

In contrast to such criticisms, proponents often identify class actions as a 'weapon of the people' against powerful social, economic and political actors. As Wendy Brown, a political

---

[3] M. Redish, 'Rethinking the Theory of the Class Action: The Risks and Rewards of Capitalistic Socialism in the Litigation Process,' (2014) 64 *Emory Law Journal* 113.

[4] ibid at 113.

[5] Even though such actions do not necessarily involve collectives as such, but can simply involve groups of similarly situated individuals and can thus be viewed more as aggregative vehicles; that is, as vehicles that aggregate individual claims.

[6] M. Redish and C.W. Berlow, 'The Class Action as Political Theory', available at http://ssrn.com/abstract=1071191.

[7] D. Rosenberg, 'Class Actions for Mass Torts: Doing Individual Justice by Collective Means,' (1987) 62 *Indiana Law Journal* 561.

theorist, has observed, class actions are 'the primary legal means by which consumers or workers band together to fight corporate abuses' and vehicles of 'organised popular power'.[8] This not only intimates towards the historical origins of the modern class action as part of desegregation campaigns in the 1960s in the Civil Rights Movement, but also implicates its continued usage as a vehicle conducive to legal mobilization efforts when the usual avenues for social and political change are not responsive.

These political tensions also extend to conceptualizations of access to justice. In a seminal study, Roderick A. Macdonald pointed out that the 'access to justice idea that ought to animate class actions proceedings is more political' than other areas of the law where individual justice-seeking predominates. Although the social and democratic benefits that stream from dispute resolution in public courts are applicable across the board, these are especially pronounced in class actions, according to Macdonald, as 'socio-economic coalitions can deploy [them] to effect changes in government policy'.[9] The politics of the procedure, then, often rooted in the interests of actors who do not wish to be held liable for their misconduct, also implicates broader concerns about the purpose of the courts, fears of judicial overreach (whether unfounded or not), and the democratic legitimacy of using 'law as politics by other means'.[10]

---

[8] Brown has observed that class actions 'have long been crucial instruments of worker and consumer resistance to discriminatory, deceptive, or fraudulent corporate behaviour, from underpaying and overcharging to polluting or violating health and safety laws', W. Brown, 'Law and Legal Reason,' in *Undoing the Demos* (New York, NY: Zone Books, 2015) at 152–4.

[9] R. Macdonald, 'Access to Justice in Canada Today' in J. Bass, W.A. Bogart and F.H. Zemans (eds), *Access to Justice for a New Century: The Way Forward* (Toronto: Law Society of Upper Canada, 2005) at 51.

[10] Concerns which, again, tend to fall along political lines, although not as clearly demarcated as in the class action context.

Given that the modern class action is a civil procedure, a chief field in which this political tension has found expression is in debates over procedural rules. For the average onlooker observing civil procedural reform processes from the outside, there is outsized debate over what may appear to be tiny differences and obscure rules – opt-in vs opt-out mechanisms; cost-shifting rules; standing requirements; types of damages available; distribution programmes; and so forth. This, however, has been a main battleground in the retrenchment of access to justice, lending credence to E.E. Schattschneider's famous dictum that 'the rules of the game determine the requirements of success'.[11] The politics of the procedure are perhaps most obvious when public consultations are held during such reform processes. A simple glance at the organizations and interests who submit materials during such processes gives an informative overview of the lie of the land.

It is easy enough to demonstrate how politics have shaped civil litigation in the United States, where civil litigation has emerged as a prominent topic in political elections and partisan debate, more so than in perhaps any other state.[12] It might therefore be more edifying to examine the role of such politicization in other regimes. Take, for instance, the recent public consultation held by the Law Commission of Ontario in its 25-year review of that province's class action regime, where the

---

[11] E.E. Schattschneider (1892–1971) as quoted by Sarah Staszak in *No Day in Court: Access to Justice and the Politics of Judicial Retrenchment* (Oxford: Oxford University Press, 2015) at 211.

[12] Given its tumultuous history and the well-established role of private litigation as a policy instrument in a multi-enforcer regulatory regime. A recurring motif in much debate in Second and Third Generation regimes has been the extent to which the United States is an 'outlier' or an 'exception' when it comes to the politicization of civil litigation, particularly class actions. S. Yeazell, *Lawsuits in a Market Economy* (Chicago, IL: University of Chicago Press, 2018).

usual suspects took their places in their respective corners, with groups representing disabled persons, low-income tenants, and environmental interests advocating in favour of strengthening the regime, and groups representing insurance companies, motor vehicle manufacturers, accounting firms, banking and commerce, and the pharmaceutical industry advocating in favour of a weakened regime. There were, of course, several submissions by prominent defence firms advocating in favour of restraint and retrenchment, and conversely, several plaintiff firms on the opposite side.[13]

Among those advocating for strengthening class actions to ensure greater access to justice were: the Advocacy Centre for Tenants Ontario, a community legal clinic promoting the interests of low-income tenants, which sought to support the adoption of class actions in administrative tribunals, such as the Landlord and Tenant Board; the Canadian Environmental Law Association, with a focus on environmental-based collective access to justice promotion; Community Living – Welland Pelham, a care community focusing on people with disabilities; and the Office of the Public Guardian and Trustee for Ontario, seeking increased access to justice for children and adults with mental disabilities. There was also representation from the litigation funding industry, such as Bentham IMF and Bridgepoint GLS.

Among those offering criticisms and seeking to restrain the scope or viability of class actions were: a conglomerate of the Big Six accounting firms (KPMG LLP; Deloitte LLP; Ernst & Young LLP; PricewaterhouseCoopers LLP; BDO Canada LLP; and MNP LLP); Canadian Vehicle Manufacturers' Association, which includes Ford Motor Company of Canada, FCA Canada Inc, and Limited and General Motors

---

[13] These included the Ad Hoc Defense Council Group, International Association of Defence Lawyers, McKenzie Lake Lawyers, Paliare Roland LLP, Rochon Genova LLP, Sotos LLP and Siskinds LLP.

of Canada Company; Canadian Bankers Association and Canadian Life and Health Insurance Association; Innovative Medicines Canada and MEDEC, a membership group of 45 companies representing the pharmaceutical industry; Insurance Bureau of Canada, a membership organization representing 90 per cent of the Canadian property and casualty insurance market; and the Ontario Chamber of Commerce. The dividing lines in the reform process are laid bare in this neat categorization of interests.[14] A similar dividing line has been present in other jurisdictions, including England and Wales.

It may come as a surprise that this latter group also featured a submission from outside Canada, from the US Chamber of Commerce's Institute for Legal Reform, a leading advocacy organization in the conservative legal movement. A central feature of this movement since the 1970s and into the early decades of the 21st century has been its increasingly global reach. What was once a conservative retrenchment against civil litigation in the United States has now been globalized in no small part due to the proliferation of class actions as legal transplants. Such efforts have also been evident in England and Wales, despite its relatively modest inroads into class actions and collective mechanisms.

---

[14] The Law Commission of Ontario's Final Report offered a relatively balanced set of recommendations, largely in favour of strengthening the regime and promoting collective access to justice, only for the Conservative government of Doug Ford to turn around and introduce the most far-reaching retrenchment of access to justice in Ontario in a generation, the Smarter and Stronger Justice Act, which undercut legal aid provisioning and services, in addition to weakening the province's class action regime (by, for instance, introducing predominance and superiority criteria at certification) – a retrenchment that was so severe that it prompted a stern reply from the Law Commission of Ontario, as well as a host of legal aid and access to justice groups.

Contesting legal narratives

One of the defining features of class action reforms has been the extent to which the debate has been politicized with questionable ideas. Tropes of a compensation culture, abusive litigation, fat-cat lawyers, blackmail suits, growing adversariality and endemic litigiousness that will have negative social repercussions have coloured the debate and come to be treated as received wisdom, despite the absence of a robust evidence base.[15] In the social production of legal knowledge, as William Haltom and Michael McCann have observed, polemical treatises, 'common sense' rhetoric, and 'tort tales' reinforced by mass media narratives are often more effective in shaping public discourse than academic scholarship.[16] The moral panic generated in the popular press (often widely read tabloids such as *The Daily Mail* and *The Sun*) by sensationalized articles describing a rampant compensation culture in the United Kingdom can have far more pervasive and long-lasting impact than any number of sober empirical studies in academic journals that demonstrate the baselessness of the fear, even at the point of policy formation and legal reform.[17]

---

[15] This appears to be the case even for those in positions of authority and power. As one senior justice stakeholder observed: "I'm of two minds about it, truth be told. The cynical part of me thinks that they're parroting the talking points given to them by their higher-ups, really don't know much about it and don't care to either. It's not a hill they're willing to die on. It's not something voters care about. That's probably the case. The other part of me thinks that they genuinely believe we'll suddenly turn into USA 2.0. I don't know which one is worse." Respondent 5, interviewed on 1 December 2018.

[16] W. Haltom and M. McCann, *Distorting the Law: Politics, Media, and the Litigation Crisis* (Chicago, IL: University of Chicago Press, 2004).

[17] See, eg, J. Hand, 'The Compensation Culture: Cliché or Cause for Concern?' (2010) 37(4) *Journal of Law and Society* 569–91; E. Quill and R.J. Friel (eds), *Damages and Compensation Culture: Comparative Perspectives* (Oxford: Hart Publishing, 2016); K. Williams, 'State of Fear: Britain's Compensation Culture Reviewed' (2005) 25(3) *Legal Studies: The Journal of the Society of Legal Scholars* 499–514. The trope of a 'compensation culture'

What is needed, as Haltom and McCann note, is to balance the critical empirical scholarship with normative, interpretative research to address this discursive mismatch.[18]

Although part of a broader popular narrative about law – featuring the vilification of lawyers, sensational tales of individuals who seek to capitalize on the slightest incurred harm for a payday, and critiques of the use of litigation itself as an 'anti-democratic politics' by other means – class actions have been spotlighted as emblematic of the type of litigation culture (and the type of entrepreneurial lawyering) found in the United States[19] and which 'respectable' legal regimes (for example England and Wales) should seek to avoid at all costs.

This is not a recent phenomenon. Contesting legal narratives have been part and parcel of the class action story. As legal historian David Marcus has observed:

> Depending on who tells it, it is either a story of good-hearted private citizens riding to the rescue of vulnerable communities injured by corporate behemoths, or a tale of massive corruption engineered by lawyer parasites. It is a story of scrappy lawyer underdogs driven by a mixture of ego, money, and righteous indignation as they assault corporate goliaths. It is a story of deregulation, of the

---

has been extensively discussed in Parliament as well, with the Better Regulation Task Force (BRTF) determining that there was no such thing and several MPs, including David Lammy (Labour) noting that those 'in positions of responsibility should not talk up a compensation culture' as the BRTF recommended, while encouraging the media to not do so as well. HC Deb (07 September 2004) vol. 424, available at https://hansard.parliament.uk/Commons/2004-09-07/debates/3d71521e-687e-4f53-9b9b-f9db57f69723/CompensationCulture?highlight=%22compensation%20culture%22#contribution-7e9006cc-2a2f-4b4a-9c11-7a97d74ddd15.

[18] Haltom and McCann (n 16) at 110. In some ways, this book speaks to this call.

[19] Well-functioning regimes like those in Canada and Australia are usually ignored in favour of American developments.

Civil Rights Movement's ebbs and flows, of the perils of a mass consumer society, of judicial activism, of HIV, of tobacco, and of Wall Street greed. It is a capitalism story about the commodification of law enforcement.[20]

It is a complicated story, to be sure. The fora for this discourse have been both mass media outputs and various lobbying efforts (from private meetings with legislators to media campaigns and public submissions to influence law reform processes), all with varying degrees of success. This has not only been evident in First and Second Generation regimes that we have discussed so far, but also in Third Generation regimes like England and Wales where, as John Peysner has observed, it 'is clear that the government has responded to lobbying and dipping its toe in the water by steering what it saw as a middle course between compensating victims and generating litigation'.[21] Among its proposed 'safeguards', Justice Not Profit, an advocacy body of the US Chamber of Commerce's Institute for Legal Reform that has been active in the United Kingdom, recommends implementing stringent class certification standards, preserving the 'loser pays' principle, favouring opt-in over opt-out models, strict standing requirements, restricting contingency fees, regulating third party litigation funding (and banning its use in class actions), and banning punitive damages. Each of these proposals, to varying extents, has been accepted in England and Wales.[22] With this in mind, we can now take a closer look at developments in this jurisdiction in recent years.

---

[20] D. Marcus, 'The History of the Modern Class Action, Part I: Sturm und Drang, 1953–1980' (2013) 90(3) *Washington University Law Review* 592.

[21] J. Peysner, 'Playing the Man not the Ball' in W.H. Van Boom (ed), *Litigation, Costs, Funding and Behaviour: Implications for the Law* (London: Routledge, 2017) at 67.

[22] The third party litigation funding industry is still largely self-regulated and the Competition Appeal Tribunal class action operates on an opt-in/opt-out model.

Collective actions in England and Wales

We have seen how the idea of representative litigation is not a new phenomenon but rather dates back to the medieval period. Far from being a radical departure imported from the United States as a legal transplant, the roots of the legal tradition are actually found in England. We also saw how, despite other common law regimes identifying the shortcomings of the representative rule and introducing new procedures for collective claims, the same reforms have not been undertaken in England and Wales on the same scale. It is thus worthwhile to take a closer look at the reform efforts in this jurisdiction since the late 1980s. These can be grouped into three stages: a period covering 1987 to 2004, one covering 2004 to 2010, and a third covering 2010 to the present day.[23]

First period of reforms (1987–2004)

The first period began in earnest with a series of cases in the late 1980s and early 1990s that exposed the limitations of the existing options, including the representative action, but also other commonly used measures such as joinder, test cases and consolidation. Cases involving environmental claims, product liability, pharmaceutical and medical harms, and mass transport disasters, to name but a few, highlighted the need for a new procedure to deal with such collective justiciable problems in an effective and efficient manner. These included cases involving: a vaccine that caused neurological harm in children (the 'whooping cough' vaccination litigation); an anti-arthritis drug

---

[23] This periodization owes a debt to J. Sorabji, 'Collective Action Reform in England and Wales' in D. Fairgrieve and E. Lein (eds), *Extraterritoriality and Collective Redress, Part I – Collective Redress Mechanisms in a Comparative Perspective* (Oxford: Oxford University Press, 2012) at 43–66; D. Grave, M. McIntosh and G. Rowan (eds), *Class Actions in England and Wales* (London: Sweet & Maxwell, 2018).

that allegedly caused onycholysis and other ailments (the Opren litigation); contaminated NHS blood products that infected 300 haemophiliacs with HIV (brought against the Department of Health); a spinal cord injection that caused arachnoiditis (the Myodil litigation); addiction arising out of the use of benzodi-azepine tranquilizers; a contraceptive that was implanted into women that caused severe side-effects (the Norplant litigation); and lung cancer claims arising out of tobacco use.[24]

As some pointed out at the time, cases had been brought against the same defendants in other jurisdictions, notably the United States, with class actions, while in England and Wales claimants had been left with an inadequate array of procedural measures that limited their capacities to access justice.[25] Among the subsequent calls for reform, including a 1988 Civil Justice Review, was a call to examine how such procedures had operated in other jurisdictions.[26] Although there was some judicial ini-tiative during this period to liberalize court rules to allow for a more flexible approach to collective claims, particularly in the context of the representative action, this was largely unsuccessful and culminated in a judicial call for legislative action.[27] At that

---

[24] For a good overview, see Grave et al (n 23) at 18–23.

[25] Sir John Donaldson noted in *Davies v Eli Lilly* (1987):

[I]n some jurisdictions, notably the United States, where large numbers of plaintiffs are making related claims against the same defendants, there are special procedures laid down enabling all the claims to be disposed of in a single action. Clearly this is some-thing which should be looked at by the appropriate authorities with a view to seeing whether it has anything to offer and, if so, introducing the necessary procedural rules.

Quoted in Sorabji (n 23) at 45.

[26] This is the type of research conducted by Rachael Mulheron in a report submitted to the Civil Justice Council in 2008.

[27] Purchas LJ observed in *Nash v Eli Lilly & Co*: '[T]here may well be a strong case for legislative action to provide a jurisdictional structure for the collation and resolution of mass product liability claims, particularly

point, whatever chance, whether realistic or advisable, for courts to undertake the major reform necessary to tackle the problem had been extinguished. It was now up to the legislature to implement the reforms. That Lord Woolf had thereafter been tasked to undertake a major review of access to justice in the English civil justice system was a fortuitous development. This resulted in a series of recommendations for multi-party actions in Lord Woolf's seminal *Final Report on Access to Justice* in 1996.

In contrast to other common law countries, Lord Woolf observed, there is a need for new procedures in England and Wales to address this gap, as First and Second Generation regimes had done in their respective jurisdictions.[28] The new procedures, accordingly, had to be designed with the following objectives in mind: first and foremost, to 'provide access to justice where large numbers of people have been affected by another's conduct, but individual loss is so small that it makes individual action economically unviable'.[29] This objective speaks to the ways in which opt-out class actions can promote access to justice for those with negative value claims. In contrast to this objective, the second objective of the reforms was to 'provide expeditious, effective and proportionate methods of resolving cases, where individual damages are large enough to justify individual action but where the number of claimants and the nature of the issues involved mean that the cases cannot be managed satisfactorily in accordance with normal procedure'.[30] This speaks to the case management concerns that pervaded the Final Report. The third and final objective of reforms was to 'achieve a balance between the normal rights of claimants and defendants, to pursue and defend cases individually, and

---

in the pharmaceutical field, but this court cannot devise such rules', quoted in Sorabji (n 23) at 46.

[28] Rt Hon. Lord Woolf, *Final Report to the Lord Chancellor on the Civil Justice System in England and Wales* (HMSO, July 1996) at ch 17.

[29] ibid at 2(a).

[30] ibid at 2(b).

the interests of a group of parties to litigate the action as a whole in an effective manner'.[31]

Following on from the Final Report, the Group Litigation Order Regime ('GLO regime') was implemented in 2000.[32] The GLO regime speaks to the second objective identified by Lord Woolf. It provides a case management framework for managing individual claims in cases that give rise to common or related issues of fact or law. At the time of writing, there have been approximately 109 GLOs according to statistics published by Her Majesty's Courts and Tribunals Service.[33] A wide variety of cases have been advanced as GLOs, including claims involving child abuse, environmental harms, data breaches, employment issues and financial misconduct. Importantly, the GLO is not a representative action: individual claims are grouped together, but there is no representative acting on behalf of all claimants. The relatively limited use of the GLO is likely a reflection of its purpose as a regime that allows for the efficient and effective management of a group of similar individual claims, operating on the requirement that each claimant must advance their claim individually at first instance, whether by initiating litigation or joining the group register.

The purpose of the GLO is less to promote accessible justice for those who would not otherwise pursue their claims and more to allow for those who have already pursued their claims to do so as a group. For its stated purposes, then, the GLO regime can be said to be functioning as well as can reasonably be expected. The same cannot be said from the perspective of Lord Woolf's first objective: that of promoting access to justice for those for whom individual action is not viable. To put it in plain language: the GLO regime does not open the doors

---

[31] ibid at 2(c).

[32] Civil Procedure Rules, r 19.10.

[33] It is important to note that these statistics are not comprehensive. 'Group Litigation Orders', available at https://www.gov.uk/guidance/group-litigation-orders.

of justice for those who cannot enter; it organizes the claims of those who have already entered.

It was not long before the limitations of the GLO regime were recognized. Within a year of its implementation, another reform process began: in 2001, the Lord Chancellor's Department undertook a consultation that sought to address the low-value claims that Lord Woolf had identified as constituting an unmet legal need and which were not covered in the GLO regime.[34] What was needed was a procedure that was opt-out in nature (given that the claims to be addressed were low value and an opt-in regime would be ineffectual in capturing all claimants) and obviously generic, as civil procedure must be – that is, would apply across the breadth of substantive law rather than only apply to a single sector or substantive area. Recognizing that rational low-value claimants would not have sufficient incentives to properly monitor an action or otherwise act as a guardian of the interests of class members, the 2001 Consultation Paper also proposed that a representative body could advance claims on behalf of a class of claimants.[35] The paper recognized precisely the type of justiciable problems that a generic opt-out class action regime would cover, and sought to implement a form of such an action. Despite support from justice stakeholders, the Labour Government of Tony Blair

---

[34] Lord Chancellor's Department, *Representative Claims: Proposed New Procedures* (2001) available at http://webarchive.nationalarchives.gov.uk/.

[35] This latter feature – also sometimes called an 'ideological claimant' as the body does not necessarily have an interest in the claim, but is rather acting in the interests of claimants – can be a promising addition to a collective action landscape (often requiring a relaxation to standing requirements), but only if it does not come at the expense of claimants being able to advance claims on their own behalf as well; otherwise the requirement of a representative body can be viewed as simply another barrier faced by justice-seekers, which is perhaps why defendant lobby groups have often advocated in favour of requiring a representative body in order to advance an action (where reform is unavoidable) as such a requirement has a chilling effect on prospective litigation.

elected not to pursue the necessary reform, citing, among other reasons, reservations about the opt-out nature of the proposal.[36]

In its place, the Enterprise Act 2002 was introduced. This was a reform that allowed a representative body to advance a claim on behalf of a class of claimants, but only on an opt-in basis and only in the CAT. The claim could also not be advanced on a 'stand-alone basis', that is, arising organically from an incurred harm without the intervention of a public body (this basis is optimal as it removes the requirement for a prior decision establishing liability). Any action, under the new regime, could only be advanced on a 'follow-on basis', meaning that a regulator would have to first decide that an infringement had occurred. This was a severe requirement intended to prevent frivolous or abusive litigation, a common refrain in class action discourse, as actions needed to go through a prior screening process of sorts. That the regime still only allowed for opt-in actions, despite this requirement, can be viewed (generously) as indicative of an over-cautious or con-servative approach to reform.

The glaring criticism, then, was that this was a pale substi-tute for what could have been meaningful and robust reform to address the access to justice gap – a criticism that proved accurate: only a single claim was advanced under the new regime, taken forward by Which? as the designated representa-tive body against JJB Sports for overcharging for replica football shirts. This was a follow-on action from a prior decision by the Office of Fair Trading. Despite the claim potentially covering over a million people, only a fraction of those claimants ever received any compensation given the opt-in nature of the regime: 130 claimants opted into the action, with the total amount recovered amounting to roughly £21,000. This was

---

[36] Concerns were also raised about the aggregation of damages and the legitimacy of a representative body acting on behalf of claimants without having any direct interest in the claim itself.

less than 1 per cent of the total claim value and total potential claimants. If that were not enough of a blow, after the action Which? declared that it would no longer act as a representative body in light of the experience. The new regime was not fit for purpose. One senior stakeholder put it plainly: "it was an unmitigated disaster."[37]

It was only a matter of time before the new regime would fall into disuse, given these limitations, yet the most far-reaching repercussion in response to the 2001 Consultation Paper was the decision by the government to move forward on reforms on a sectoral basis, rather than on a generic basis, as recommended in the paper. "It was a deliberate attempt to slow the process down,"[38] said one stakeholder, while another added that it

'was a delaying tactic that flied [*sic*] in the face of the basic principles of civil procedure. That is not how procedural reform is enacted in this country. Procedural law is trans-substantive. We do not pick and choose [between sectors or substantive areas]. If you needed any hard evidence that the government had no intention of enacting meaningful reform, that was it.'[39]

A more generous interpretation took this perspective on board, noting that

'of course there's a problem in that, generally speaking, we do not take the view and haven't taken the view since the 1870s that procedure should be substantive law specific. But that type of procedural perspective is not found within government ... the actual trans-substantivity of procedural law is not really a factor that's thought about.'[40]

---

[37] Respondent 28, interview on 7 November 2019.
[38] Respondent 15, interview on 24 January 2019.
[39] Respondent 17, interview on 1 March 2019.
[40] Respondent 28, interview on 7 November 2019.

Irrespective of the reason why the sectoral approach was adapted, a consensus among stakeholders was that once this approach was determined as the proper course moving forward, the scope of future reforms was severely limited (by design).[41]

Second period of reforms (2004–10)

Responding to the failure of the first period of reform activity, what can be viewed as the second period began in earnest in 2004. This period, too, was one of disappointment. As John Sorabji has observed, 'the six years from 2004–10 were full of sound and fury, which ultimately signified nothing'.[42] Given the 'most conservative possible' reform of the earlier period, advocates may have been forgiven for thinking that things could not possibly get any worse, but the second period did not even produce a reform as patently unfit for purpose as the first: it did not produce a single reform.[43]

There was, however, a steady growth of activity that laid the groundwork for reforms, such as research and consultations, signalling an increasing awareness that the significant gaps in civil justice for collective access remained unaddressed. In 2005 the Department of Trade & Industry published a strategy consultation report announcing that collective action reform was forthcoming for consumer claims, with the support of consumer groups, regulators and Trading Standards organizations.[44]

---

[41] While some respondents observed that this does not rule out a generic regime at some point in the future, others outright rejected the possibility of anything other than the present sectoral approach.

[42] Sorabji (n 23) at 52.

[43] ibid.

[44] Even in this otherwise promising strategy document, the fear of a creating a 'compensation culture' and facilitating abusive or frivolous litigation was noted, as the report sought to 'avoid inadvertently creating a compensation culture and to avoid businesses facing spurious claims', Department of Trade & Industry, *A Fair Deal For All – Extending Competitive Markets: Empowered Consumers, Successful Business* (2005), at para 7.3.

The following year, the Patent Office published its 2006 consultation report in favour of introducing collective actions in the enforcement of intellectual property rights.[45] The Office of Fair Trading published a reply to the first consultation, observing that an opt-in regime would not address the access to justice gap for mass low-value claims.[46]

Interestingly, although discrimination was considered at this time as a viable sector for reform, in light of the collective nature of such harms and the social and psychological barriers faced by those most vulnerable to discrimination, such as women, LGBTQ, disabled persons, and racial and ethnic minorities, the Department of Communities and Local Government outright rejected the very idea of collective action reform.[47] During the Equality Bill debate in the Commons Chamber in December 2009, a number of MPs argued in favour of allowing the Equality and Human Rights Commission or a registered trade union to act as a representative in class actions in the bill. As Dianne Abbott (Labour) noted, class actions have been 'very effective' and '[b]y their very nature, people bringing class actions will be the lowest paid, often the most junior and marginal members of an organisation, and it is asking too much of them, as individuals, to take action one by one'.[48]

---

[45] Patent Office, *Representative Actions for the Enforcement of Intellectual Property Rights* (Patent Office, 2006).

[46] Office of Fair Trading, *Representative Actions in Consumer Protection Legislation – Department for Trade and Industry: A Consultation Response* (Office of Fair Trading, 2006).

[47] Department of Communities and Local Government, Discrimination Law Review, *A Framework for Fairness: Proposals for a Single Equality Bill for Great Britain – A Consultation Paper* (Department of Communities and Local Government, 2007).

[48] HC Deb (2 December 2009) vol. 501, available at https://hansard. parliament.uk/Commons/2009-12-02/debates/09120237000001/ EqualityBill?highlight=%22class%20actions%22#contribution-09120237000442.

Others, such as Baroness Clark (Labour) and John McDonnell (Labour) agreed, observing that 'women workers such as cleaners, catering assistants and shop assistants' are particularly vulnerable and there is ample evidence that workers who have taken action against employers have been blacklisted as a result (at the time, over 3,000 workers, according to the Information Commissioner) who will not 'get any justice or compensation for the discrimination against them'.[49]

The Civil Justice Council took note of these developments and began, starting in 2006, a series of meetings to consider reform, commissioning an Evidence of Need study that identified a gap in collective access to justice in England and Wales that could be filled with the adoption of a generic opt-out regime that allowed for ideological claimants. The Evidence of Need study also noted, among other findings, that the employment sphere was a ripe area for reform given widespread harms, including unequal pay and discrimination claims, and that in cases involving global products that were available both in England and Wales as well as in other jurisdictions, the same products that were litigated in jurisdictions that had opt-out class action regimes had not been litigated in England and Wales.[50] This is the so-called 'missing cases' phenomenon.

In its recommendations to the Lord Chancellor,[51] the Civil Justice Council observed that the existing landscape for

---

[49] ibid. This is particularly evident in cases of unequal pay discrimination against women and racial and ethnic minorities, as noted by parliamentarians in Commons debates.

[50] R. Mulheron, *Reform of Collective Redress in England and Wales: A Perspective of Need* (Civil Justice Council, 2008).

[51] J. Sorabji, M. Napier and R. Musgrove (eds), *Improving Access to Justice through Collective Actions – Developing a More Efficient and Effective Procedure for Collective Actions – A Series of Recommendations to the Lord Chancellor* (Civil Justice Council, 2008). It also noted that such actions should be introduced in the Competition Appeal Tribunal and Employment Tribunal, that the representative parties could include individual claimants (or defendants), designated bodies, and ad hoc bodies, that such actions

collective actions was insufficient in providing access to justice for a wide range of citizens, that there was overwhelming evidence that meritorious claims were not being advanced and that these could be so advanced, more efficiently and effectively, through collective action.[52] In light of these findings, the Civil Justice Council advocated in favour of a generic class action regime that allowed for ideological claimants and that would allow for judicial discretion in determining that any given action could proceed on either an opt-in or an opt-out basis. Any prospective action would need to be certified as such, damages could be aggregated in certain cases, and any settlement would require court approval in a Fairness Hearing to ensure the protection of the interests of absent class members. It also determined that the new regime should be introduced through primary legislation given that some of the recommendations affected the substantive law.[53] A preliminary draft of a Civil Proceedings Act and Rules of Court were also included in the report, giving the clearest pathway for government to enact the necessary reforms.

The Civil Justice Council's report was rejected by the Labour government of Gordon Brown in 2009. It reiterated its commitment to a sectoral approach and repeated concerns that collective actions could result in abusive or frivolous litigation that would unfairly target and burden corporations.[54] Among its criticisms, the government took issue with the opt-out mechanism, noting that 'some consider it wrong, and likely to fuel a compensation culture for people to obtain

---

should be subject to enhanced case management by specialist judges given their complexity, that full cost shifting should obtain, and that remainders of aggregate awards should be distributed by a trustee and a cy-près distributions to a Foundation or Trust were valid.

[52] ibid at 17.

[53] ibid at 183. See also Grave et al (n 23) at 28–31.

[54] Ministry of Justice, *The Government's Response to the Civil Justice Council's Report: 'Improving Access to Justice through Collective Actions'* (Ministry of Justice, 2009).

damages having taken no positive steps to participate in an action',[55] despite those people having been harmed. Again, the ever-present trope of the 'compensation culture' that has (or will) besiege England and Wales was raised. It also stated that collective actions must be considered an option of last resort, giving preference to regulatory action and potential reform to allow for forms of regulatory redress. What had once been growing momentum that could bring forth the long-awaited reform of the collective action landscape was quickly dissipated.

Later that same month, July 2009, HM Treasury published a consultation paper on collective action reform in the financial sector.[56] In most mature regimes, claims arising out of financial markets have been among the most common types of class actions, and in the immediate aftermath of the Global Financial Crisis of 2007–8, the case for introducing such reform had become significantly stronger. It was a paper that had been drafted prior to the government's negative reply to the Civil Justice Council and eventually led to the tabling of the Financial Services Bill in Parliament in November 2009 by the Labour government. The bill included provisions for the adoption of a collective action and accepted many of the recommendations of the Civil Justice Council, including that claims could proceed on either an opt-in or opt-out basis, full costs shifting should obtain, a proceeding needed to be certified before moving forward, aggregate damages could be awarded and remainders could be distributed on a cy-près basis, and that the representative party did not need to be only a pre-designated body but could also be an individual representative claimant or another body authorized by the court.[57]

Faced with Conservative opposition to many of these features, the Financial Services Secretary to the Treasury, Lord Myners, withdrew the collective action provisions from the

---

55 ibid at 9–10.
56 HM Treasury, *Reforming Financial Markets* (HM Treasury, 2009).
57 Financial Services Bill 2009 (UK) cll. 18–25.

bill in April 2010 as a way to ensure that the bill would be passed prior to the dissolution of Parliament and the general election in May 2010. Once again, the spectre that the class action would create a 'US-style litigation culture' was raised.[58] Notably, the Labour government expressed support for the collective action provisions, observing that they were 'necessary, sensible and desirable', while the Conservative shadow justice minister suggested that it would be something for a future government to consider.[59] The Conservative Party of David Cameron thereafter won the election and formed a coalition government with the Liberal Democrats. The collective action provisions were not revisited and no such reform process has since been considered for financial services.

Third period of reforms (2010–present)

The third period has focused on reforms in competition law. This is a sector that has garnered much attention across the globe as competition law infringements often involve a large number of diffuse and fragmentary claims that are individually low value but whose total collective value can be quite high. In England and Wales, the s47B representative action was originally intended to address such claims but had fallen into disuse given its clear limitations, including that it only operated on an opt-in model and the only predesignated body that was authorized to advance cases, Which?, had taken a firm stance that it would no longer do so, as noted earlier.

---

[58] As John Howell explicitly noted during parliamentary debates on the Financial Services Bill on 30 November 2009, with Lord Darling also opposing the 'widespread development of such action, as there has been in the United States'. HC Deb (30 November 2009) vol. 501, available at: https://hansard.parliament.uk/Commons/2009-11-30/debates/09113039000001/FinancialServicesBill?highlight=%22class%20actions%22#contribution-09113039000091.

[59] Grave et al (n 23) at 32.

A new regime was thus introduced in the Competition Appeal Tribunal through the Consumer Rights Act 2015. The regime also included a set of safeguards, including a strict judicial certification stage, prohibition of contingency fees for lawyers, and full cost shifting. Despite repeated concerns by opponents about the creation of a litigation culture akin to what was perceived in the United States, the new regime learned some of the lessons of the past failure and was introduced on an opt-in/ opt-out model. The Office of Fair Trading noted that an opt-out regime would not only address the serious limitation of the s47B representative action, it would also promote deterrence, gesturing towards the positive externalities and social and economic benefits that litigation can have – consider, for instance, the potential deterrent effect that would have been exercised if JJB Sports had internalized the full costs of overcharging for replica football shirts, projected at over £160,000,000, as opposed to the £21,000 that was ultimately claimed.[60]

In its consultation in 2012, the Department for Business, Innovation and Skills agreed with the need for an opt-out regime.[61] Then Secretary of State Vince Cable observed in the government response in 2013 that not only was reforming the approach to private actions by introducing such actions a positive step in promoting fairness and access to justice for consumers who had suffered losses due to anti-competitive behaviour, but it was also beneficial for the UK economy as it would increase growth by empowering small and medium-sized businesses to take stronger action against anti-competitive behaviour, particularly by larger businesses.[62] The report

---

[60] Office of Fair Trading, *Private Actions in Competition Law: Effective Redress for Consumers and Business – Recommendations from the Office of Fair Trading* (2007).

[61] Department for Business, Innovation & Skills, *Private Actions in Competition Law: A Consultation on Options for Reform* (2012).

[62] Department for Business, Innovation & Skills, *Private Actions in Competition Law: A Consultation on Options for Reform – Government Response* (2013).

also noted that it was not practicable for such actions to be undertaken solely by public authorities given that 'they have finite resources and cannot do everything'.[63] As such, it was necessary 'to create the legal framework that will empower individual consumers and businesses to represent their own interests'.[64] The view that was endorsed, here, was that class actions also have a regulatory dimension and play a role as policy instruments in a private enforcement regime.

Once again, as with law reform processes in other jurisdictions, the forces seeking to influence the form and scope of the new regime reflected their own interests. Those seeking greater accessibility and fairness, such as the Access to Justice Foundation, Citizens Advice and a host of law centres, foundations and other actors in the access to justice space, advocated in favour of the much-needed reforms like an opt-out option to strengthen the capacities of claimants. Conversely, the usual critics of such reforms, such as various associations and corporate lobbies like the British Bankers' Association, British Chambers of Commerce, European Justice Forum and the US Chamber of Commerce's Institute for Legal Reform, resisting such changes and raising the spectre of an abusive 'litigation culture'.[65]

---

[63] ibid at 3.

[64] ibid.

[65] The full list of respondents is available in Annex C of the government's response. These included numerous actors in the access to justice space, such as Advice Centres for Avon, Advice Services Alliance, Bournemouth and Pool Pro Bono, BPP Pro Bono Centre, Brighton and Hove Advice Strategy Society, Greenwich Housing Rights, Hackney Community Law Centre, Islington Law Centre, Lambeth Law Centre, Law Centres Federation, Law for Life, LawWorks, Legal Voice, Midland Legal Support Trust, Money Advice and Community Support, North East Legal Support Trust, North Kensington Law Centre, North West Legal Support Trust, Public Law Project, Sheffield Community Law Centre, Sheffield Law Centre, Slough Immigration Aid Unit, South West Legal Support Trust, South West London Law Centres, St. Hilda's East Community Centre, Welfare Rights and Money Advice Centre, Which? and Wiltshire Law Centre.

Even as England and Wales was on the precipice of introducing the reform in 2015, the Institute for Legal Reform continued its lobbying efforts aimed at restricting the scope of the new class action (by removing the opt-out mechanism), raising the fear of frivolous litigation and runaway costs, and taking aim at the funding options for prospective claimants (focusing on third party litigation funding, addressed in the next chapter).[66] This was done under the aegis of a new organization, Justice Not Profit, backed by the US Chamber of Commerce. Despite these efforts, however, the legislation came into effect without the limitations that the corporate lobby had sought to impose. For John Peysner, the lobbying effort of Justice Not Profit 'looks like a pre-emptive strike'[67] for potential reforms in other areas.

As of 2020, it is the only sector that has introduced an opt-out class action in England and Wales. Far from opening the floodgates to abusive or frivolous litigation by unscrupulous lawyers, funders and 'compensation culture' claimants seeking to victimize businesses, only a handful of cases have been brought forward in the Competition Appeal Tribunal to date. This aligns with the experiences of similar regimes, like those in Australia and Canada: caution reigns supreme at the outset of a class action regime. It often takes several years for the actors involved – lawyers, funders, representatives, even judges – to find their footing amid the myriad complexities of such mass litigation.[68] It is one of the reasons why the sectoral approach

---

[66] For an informative analysis of the Justice Not Profit campaign in 2015, see J. Peysner, 'Playing the Man not the Ball' in W.H. Van Boom (ed), *Litigation, Costs, Funding and Behaviour: Implications for the Law* (London: Routledge, 2017) at 55–79.

[67] ibid at 68.

[68] "Nobody wants to be first out of the gate," said one senior partner. "Nice and slow wins the race, as it were. I'm quietly optimistic, but let's see what things will be like a decade from now." Respondent 8, interview on 10 December 2018.

has been viewed by some as a 'delaying tactic' as this gestation period must now likely be undergone in each sector rather than only once as in a generic regime. Others have noted that the Competition Appeal Tribunal can now serve as a test-bed for future reforms elsewhere. It remains to be seen how this class action will develop in the coming years, but it is certain that advocates for greater accessibility will be faced with a well-organized and well-funded lobbying and public campaign against any such reforms.

Finally, another area that has received increasing attention in recent years has been data protection. Indeed, Articles 80–82 of the General Data Protection Regulation (GDPR) allow for class actions since data breaches are, almost universally, mass harms. In the United Kingdom this has come to the fore particularly in the aftermath of the Cambridge Analytica scandal, Google and Apple data violations, and heightened social concerns about data privacy. 'Given the revelations about Cambridge Analytica and the fact that none of us knows whether we are included in the 50 million Facebook profiles that have been hacked,' one Labour MP noted during parliamentary debates in 2018, introducing an opt-out class action would be preferable to an opt-in model for data protection.[69] Clearly those who do not know that they have been hacked cannot logically opt into an action.

One notable ongoing case has been brought forward by Richard Lloyd (formerly of Which?) as a representative action involving the alleged tracking of personal data of 4.4 million iPhone users by Google – data that was subsequently sold to advertisers without the knowledge or consent of the users,

---

[69] HC Deb (19 March 2018) vol. 638, available at https://hansard.parliament.uk/Commons/2018-03-19/debates/2015B5CE-9F99-4B8D-B195-57C51AB4FD0C/CambridgeAnalyticaDataPrivacy?highlight=%22class%20actions%22#contribution-299543EE-D6D6-4171-B578-BEBAF2235753.

thereby violating the Data Protection Act 1998.[70] At the time of writing, the Supreme Court has granted Google permission to appeal the Court of Appeal's decision that Lloyd could act as the representative for the users. The Court of Appeal, in addition to determining that uniform per capita damages could be awarded for 'loss of control' of personal data (even without material damage, distress or pecuniary loss, given that the data has economic value), also determined that all the claimants had suffered the same loss and thus shared the 'same interest' – the criterion that has historically proven to be difficult to satisfy. The Court of Appeal also determined that a representative action was an appropriate procedure and that the claim could proceed under CPR 19.6. It remains to be seen how the Supreme Court will decide the appeal, but if the claim is allowed to proceed as such, it will be a positive step for collective access to justice in the data protection sphere.

As another Labour MP noted in the parliamentary debate on the Data Protection Bill, an opt-out procedure is especially important in the context of children's rights. The prevalent exposure of children's data (and the fact that data breaches generally do not discriminate between the ages of individual data holders, and children are active users of social media and other online activities) indicates that a representative, whether an individual or an authorized body, is necessary to bring claims on behalf of children on an opt-out basis. 'How on earth will Which? round up thousands of the nation's children to secure their positive opt-in to a class action, which it is in the national interest to bring?' asked Liam Byrne (Labour), it 'would be completely impossible'.[71] The opt-in model is 'not only weak for adults but completely ineffective for

---

[70] *Lloyd v Google LLC* [2019] EWCA Civ 1599.

[71] HC Deb (15 March 2018) vol. 637, available at: https://hansard.parliament.uk/Commons/2018-03-15/debates/3927b0fd-a500-42d8-b505-4c4b3ba83ab6/DataProtectionBill(Lords)(MorningSitting)?highlight=%22class%20actions%22#contribution-18031555000097.

children'.[72] The Conservative government, however, once again rejected the opt-out approach.

Litigation in democracy

Jurisdictions that have introduced class actions have often done so as a way of deploying the vehicle as a policy instrument in a broader private (or multi-)enforcement regime: using economic incentives to mobilize private litigation as a complement to administrative power, and in some cases as a substitute for traditional public administration.[73] This aligns with a view of class actions as involving a regulatory dimension. In this view, the class action needs to be designed in such a way as to maximize its regulatory efficacy, legitimating the role of class lawyers as 'private attorneys general'. It is a political tool in the creation of a regulatory state that is not as bureaucratically centralized and not as susceptible to regulatory capture by industry. Governments that have introduced the vehicle have also, by and large, accepted that groups of people (or businesses) can deploy it against the government itself. The United Kingdom has not permitted such accountability checks by its citizens.

For those less inclined to view law through a political lens, the class action must be viewed as strictly a procedural vehicle, the implementation of which must be cautiously approached

---

[72] ibid.

[73] For instance, during parliamentary debates over the Financial Services Bill, one MP observed that while the measures on collective redress and class actions were welcome, 'it says something about the weakness of the regulatory structure that we have to find mechanisms for consumers to hold product providers to account. Where is the FSA or the Financial Ombudsman Service failing, if we need to give consumers those powers?' HC Deb (30 November 2009) vol. 501, available at https://hansard.parliament.uk/Commons/2009-11-30/debates/09113039000001/FinancialServicesBill?highlight=%22class%20actions%22#contribution-09113039000091.

so as not to distort established norms and processes of dispute resolution. These have been the two duelling visions of class actions and they raise a central problem in conceptualizing their proper role in the civil justice system (and indeed paradigm of governance) of a democratic state.[74] Is it a strictly procedural vehicle or does it have a regulatory purpose, or are the two not mutually exclusive? Where the class action is deployed as a policy instrument in a multi-enforcer regime, it can generate problems of 'democratic accountability', and where it is strictly a procedural vehicle it can 'lose some of its regulatory force'.[75]

To the extent that regulatory agencies can offer solutions for the mass justiciable problems in a jurisdiction, these can be viewed as viable alternatives to private recourse to law and private enforcement. Public regulators can, for instance, be better positioned than private enforcers to acquire information about the extent of the harms incurred and the identity of victims.[76] Yet there are long-standing issues with relying on regulatory action, including the absence or limitations of regulatory redress, which effectively means that individuals and groups would not receive any compensation for their incurred harms, as well as the potential for regulatory capture by industry and reluctance by regulators to pursue certain types of cases.[77] '[I]f public enforcers had the resources and willingness both to prosecute culpable defendants, and to pursue compensatory redress on behalf of victims of that behaviour,' Mulheron

---

[74] Marcus (n 20) at 5.

[75] ibid at 6–7.

[76] It is beyond the scope of this book to engage fully in the debates over private and public enforcement. See, eg, C. Hodges and S. Voet, *Delivering Collective Redress: New Technologies* (Oxford: Hart Publishing, 2018); K. Huschelrath and H. Schweitzer (eds), *Public and Private Enforcement of Competition Law in Europe: Legal and Economic Perspectives* (London: Springer, 2014).

[77] The promise of such regulatory intervention has been championed by corporate lobby groups as a strategic intervention against the adoption of class actions.

has observed, 'then the need for private enforcement via civil litigation would be reduced, if not obviated.'[78] That public enforcers have not 'fulfil[led] that role has been a key trigger in promoting opt-out class action reform'.[79]

In many ways the debate over class actions can be viewed as part of the broader debate over the role of private litigation in a democratic polity. The increasing role of courts and litigation in the political sphere has drawn fierce criticism from different quarters, not least of which are those who view recourse to law, particularly as a means of effecting social change and holding powerful actors to account, as an undemocratic encroachment into parliamentary supremacy.[80] These critics have typically raised the spectre of 'unelected activist judges' usurping the powers of the legislature and expanding the empire of law at the expense of representative democracy.[81] The perceived rise of judicial power and an emergent 'juristocracy' has not only served to legalize politics, but has also politicized law, both to the detriment of democratic politics and parliamentary government, in this view, pitting 'the people' against the judiciary,

---

[78] R. Mulheron, *Class Actions and Government* (Cambridge: Cambridge University Press, 2020) at 72.

[79] ibid.

[80] Irrespective of the efficacy of deploying the law for such purposes or the repercussions inherent in the legalization of social movement activity. See, eg, G. Rosenberg, *The Hollow Hope: Can Courts Bring About Social Change?* 2nd edition (Chicago, IL: University of Chicago Press, 2008); M. McCann, *Rights at Work: Pay Equity Reform and the Politics of Legal Mobilization* (Chicago, IL: University of Chicago Press, 1994).

[81] In the United Kingdom, a notable conservative purveyor of this line of criticism has been the Judicial Power Project, launched in 2015. Notable figures in this jurisdiction that have endorsed this view include Lord Sumption, former Justice of the Supreme Court. See, eg, his Reith Lectures, published and expanded in J. Sumption, *Trials of the State: Law and the Decline of Politics* (London: Profile Books, 2019); see also R. Ekins, P. Yowell and N.W. Barber, *Lord Sumption and the Limits of the Law* (Oxford: Bloomsbury, 2018).

with the latter identified as the 'enemy' of the former.[82] To the extent that the modern class action has been a critical innovation that has empowered people to use the law in seeking justice, whichever form this may take (whether compensation, deterrence, or broader social change), it has often been viewed as emblematic of the anti-democratic expansion of judicial power.[83] Its origins as a vehicle of legal mobilization in the Civil Rights Movement and its continued use in similar cases has made it a lightning rod for such critiques.

Other scholars have disputed the existence of rampant judicial activism, reaffirming the role of courts as democratic institutions and the constitutional principle of judicial independence as a cornerstone of a democracy governed by the rule of law.[84] Litigation is understood here as a vital and necessary component of democratic life, and as a form of citizen

---

[82] J. Rozenberg, *Enemies of the People? How Judges Shape Society* (Bristol: Bristol University Press, 2020). The title of the book (which effectively dismantles this view) is taken from the infamous *Daily Mail* headline identifying judges as the 'enemies of the people' on 4 November 2016. This was not confined to right-wing tabloids, as *The Telegraph* also featured a similar front page of 'Judges vs the People' on the same date in response to a perceived anti-Brexit judicial decision.

[83] While it is beyond the scope of this book to examine this debate in the detail it warrants, it is nevertheless worthwhile to observe that the rise of the juristocracy is less a result of activist judges usurping power from the legislature, as Ran Hirschl observes, and more an outcome of political actors seeking to deflect and shift responsibility to the courts over pressing and often controversial topics, thereby seeking to avoid public blame and voter backlash. R. Hirschl, *Towards Juristocracy: The Origins and Consequences of the New Constitutionalism* (Cambridge, MA: Harvard University Press, 2004).

[84] See, eg, A. Lahav, *In Praise of Litigation* (Oxford: Oxford University Press, 2017); S. Farhang, *The Litigation State: Public Regulation and Private Lawsuits in the US* (Princeton, NJ: Princeton University Press, 2010); H. Genn, *Judging Civil Justice* (The Hamlyn Lectures) (Cambridge: Cambridge University Press, 2010); A. Paterson, *Lawyers and the Public Good: Democracy in Action?* (The Hamlyn Lectures) (Cambridge: Cambridge University Press, 2011).

empowerment and self-government, with public courts as fora of democratic deliberation. The civil justice system can be viewed as a legitimate space in the development of public policy, with access to its institutions being a matter of principle as well as a matter of broader importance for the well-being of a polity given the positive externalities that judicial adjudication can offer for social order, stability and economic activity.

If anything, the juridification of the social sphere in the post-war period – referring to the ever-increasing range of everyday social experiences and relations that have become subject to legal regulation, partly as a result of the establishment of the welfare state, the increasing availability of legal remedies for incurred harms, and the devaluation of other norm-generating social fields – has given rise to concerns about the capacity of people to navigate the juridified lifeworlds in which they find themselves. Empowering people to enforce their rights and protect their interests, that is, promoting access to justice, takes on heightened significance in this context, and procedures that are conducive to such empowerment, such as the class action, should therefore be embraced. This is why retrenchment efforts, particularly those aimed at class actions, have been characterized by political theorists as forms of 'de-democratisation', which refers to a broader phenomenon involving the substantive 'hollow[ing] out [of] the practices and institutions of liberal democracy'.[85] In this view, far from recourse to law and courts being anti-democratic intrusions into politics, it is rather efforts that seek

---

[85] W. Brown, 'Law and Legal Reason' in *Undoing the Demos* (New York, NY: Zone Books, 2015) at 153–4. For a detailed exploration of the various facets of de-democratization, see W. Brown, 'We Are All Democrats Now ...' in G. Agamben, A. Badiou, D. Bensaid, W. Brown, J Nancy, J. Ranciere, K. Ross and S. Žižek (eds), *Democracy in What State?* (New York, NY: Columbia University Press, 2011) at 44–57. See also S. Staszak, *No Day In Court: Access to Justice and the Politics of Judicial Retrenchment* (Oxford: Oxford University Press, 2015).

to unduly restrict access to justice that are anti-democratic in nature, including attacks on class actions that amount to attempts to disempower vulnerable people by restricting the procedural mechanisms that give effect to substantive rights and entitlements.

Compensation and deterrence

A key controversy in this debate has been the difficulties in balancing the objectives of compensation and deterrence. The tension between these objectives has extended to the terminological terrain. There has been a strong push by critics of class actions to reframe the debate over new collective procedures as 'collective redress' mechanisms rather than 'collective actions' or 'class actions'. Whereas the latter typically involve litigation and incorporate the dual objectives of compensation and deterrence (as well as judicial economy, in some cases), the former term prioritizes compensation (re: redress) which does not have to be accomplished through litigation in public courts, but can also be accomplished, to varying degrees, through ADR mechanisms.

This tension is also evident in the context of distributing awards. In an opt-out regime, given the relatively low value of the claims in most cases, there is generally a low take-up rate – that is, the rate at which class members make claims for compensation.[86] This may be due to apathy or ignorance of ongoing actions, the difficulty or impossibility of identifying class members, or the impracticality of distributing relatively small amounts to class members (in cases where costs of distribution outweigh the value of distributable funds). Whichever

---

[86] This can be addressed in various ways, such as improving notice practices that notify class members that they may be due compensation (by using plain language rather than legalese, distributing notices online and in targeted ways, and so forth).

the cause, there is often a sizable remainder of the award left over that has not been claimed. How should such unclaimed sums be distributed?

Unsurprisingly, defendant lobby groups usually argue that this remainder should revert back to the defendants. This can also be viewed as aligning with the compensatory principle that underscores most civil justice damages, as the government noted in its rejection of the Civil Justice Council's 2008 recommendation, adding that any surplus must revert to the defendants, otherwise it would be 'unfair to defendants' and might even be considered 'punitive'.[87] Among the problems, however, with such funds simply reverting back to defendants is that it fails to ensure that wrongdoers have internalized the costs of their wrongdoing and the full deterrent effect of the litigation is lost.

One solution to this dilemma is to identify a pre-authorized recipient of any unclaimed sums. That is precisely the approach taken in the Competition Law Class Action, with the Access to Justice Foundation identified as the optimal recipient – an organization that received widespread support in the government consultation from the legal aid and advice sector, as well as from The Law Society of England and Wales, among others. Subject to court approval, any unclaimed sums can be distributed to the Access to Justice Foundation, given the purpose of class actions as promoting access to justice. Another viable solution is to introduce cy-près distributions. The concept of cy-près refers to the principle of 'as near as possible' and in the case of distributions, can be applied to distribute unclaimed funds in ways that would most closely benefit class members (re: 'as near as possible' or 'the next best' form of distribution). So rather than a single pre-authorized body benefiting from all unclaimed sums, the court can have wide discretion to allocate those sums to recipients that may be more directly

---

[87] Ministry of Justice (n 54) at 12.

relevant to the action.[88] For instance, in a class action over employment discrimination, the unclaimed sums could go to an organization that specializes in tackling discrimination in the workplace. Finally, an escheat distribution may also be appropriate, although this should be considered only in exceptional circumstances. This entails the unclaimed sums being awarded to the state. In reform consultations in England and Wales, the potential of the Treasury being a designated recipient for escheat distributions has been raised.[89] Deputizing private actions by government (in line with a civil fine framework) would find its clearest expression in such an arrangement. Notably, this has been strongly opposed by government and stakeholders, who have been almost unanimous in support of the unclaimed funds being used for purposes relevant to the underlying drivers of the litigation, including promoting access to justice.[90]

The reason why questions over distributions implicate the role of litigation in a democracy is because it can reorient the basic remedial structure in favour of deterrence and transform the traditional compensatory principle underpinning civil justice into something akin to civil fines.[91] This reorientation

---

[88] This does require judicial scrutiny to ensure the appropriateness of the cy-près recipient.

[89] Department for Business, Innovation & Skills, *Private Actions in Competition Law: A Consultation on Options for Reform – Government Response*, January 2013 at 5.66.

[90] ibid at 5.67.

[91] While it must be recognized that class members do not always want monetary outcomes – justice is not reducible to money, and victims often seek social recognition of loss, public apologies, medical and educational programmes, and cessation of wrongful activity – it is beyond the scope of this book to delve into the 'compensationalist hegemony' that prevails in traditional civil justice approaches. This is a term used by Miriam Gilles and Gary B. Friedman to describe the insistence on prioritizing direct compensation to class members over other social benefits, including deterring future misconduct, in class action policy and scholarship. M. Gilles and G.B. Friedman, 'Exploding the Class Action Agency Costs Myth: The Social Utility of Entrepreneurial Lawyers' (2006) 155 *University of Pennsylvania Law Review* 108.

can be viewed as the culmination of the regulatory conception of class actions as policy instruments in private enforcement regimes. By introducing a third party who stands to benefit from the litigation, this 'trilateralization of the bilateral adjudicatory process', critics argue, serves the 'redistribution of wealth for social good'.[92] To take a generous interpretation, this is perceived to be illegitimate as a matter of principle rather than outcome. Although this author does concur with The Law Society of England and Wales and the plethora of access to justice organizations who accept the legitimacy of such distributions, particularly to a body such as the Access to Justice Foundation, this is an important facet in the design of a class action regime that warrants greater attention moving forward as it raises fundamental questions about the purpose of the civil justice system.

Conclusion

What is clear from this discussion is that the effort to introduce the 'new procedures' that Lord Woolf advocated have not been a straightforward endeavour. Perhaps more than most areas of justice reform, collective access to justice is a field of contestation between competing social, economic and political forces, including corporate lobby and policy advocacy groups seeking to limit the financial exposure of potential defendants by advocating for strict limitations where class actions have been adopted or their adoption has been under debate. This has also involved discursive forays attacking potential claims-makers as seeking to capitalize on the slightest incurred harms in the trope of a 'compensation culture' and broader political attacks on the legitimacy of litigation in a democratic state. In

---

[92] M. Redish, P. Julian and S. Zyontz, 'Cy Pres Relief and the Pathologies of the Modern Class Action: A Normative and Empirical Analysis' (2010) 62(3) *Florida Law Review* 642.

the class action context, much criticism has centred on the role of economic motivations and the rise of entrepreneurial litigation. As the next chapter outlines, this has largely focused on the role of private legal actors, such as lawyers and third party funders, who pursue mass litigation for private economic gain.

FOUR

Understanding the Economics
of Class Actions

When Lord Woolf laid out the first of the three main objectives of the 'new procedures' that are needed for dealing with group interests in the Final Report on Access to Justice in 1996, he was effectively making an economic argument for the access to justice benefits of opt-out class actions. The first objective is to 'provide access to justice where large numbers of people have been affected by another's conduct, but individual loss is so small that it makes individual action economically unviable'.[1] With this in mind, this chapter offers an accessible framework for understanding the economics of class actions. It outlines some key concepts and economic enablers that allow for mass litigation, focusing on claimants, lawyers and funders (both private and public). This is based on the recognition that the most important aspect of a class action regime is its economic viability. Before delving further, however, a brief background on this approach is warranted.

---

[1]   Rt Hon. Lord Woolf, *Final Report to the Lord Chancellor on the Civil Justice System in England and Wales* (HMSO, July 1996) at ch 17.2(a).

Economic analysis of law

The economic analysis of law has come under scrutiny from across the legal and political spectrum. Although this approach – what has come to be known as the 'law and economics' methodology – has become a mainstream movement in American legal research, this enthusiasm has not been shared in England and Wales. Critics have raised concerns about the legal implications and political biases of the movement, its funding sources, its assumptions rooted in neoclassical economics, and its role in the conservative legal movement from the 1970s onwards.[2] Notable potent criticisms have been raised over central tenets such as the primacy of efficiency as a normative ideal, the optimality of outcomes produced in competitive 'free' markets, and wealth maximization being a primary social good. One overarching criticism has been the movement's perceived economism; that is, the overvaluing of economic metrics, methodologies and theory, and a concomitant subordination and reduction of social reality to the same.[3] This author shares these concerns.

---

[2] See, eg, S. Teles, *The Rise of the Conservative Legal Movement: The Battle for Control of the Law* (Princeton, NJ: Princeton University Press, 2010); J. Kwak, 'Law and Economism' (2018) 5(1) *Critical Analysis of Law* 39; R. Dworkin, 'Is Wealth a Value?' (1980) 9 *Journal of Legal Studies* 191; A.T. Kronman, 'Wealth Maximization as a Normative Principle' (1980) 9 *Journal of Legal Studies* 227; G. Minda, 'Towards a More "Just" Economics of Justice – A Review Essay' (1989) 10 *Cardozo Law Review* 1855; R.P. Malloy, 'Invisible Hand or Sleight of Hand? Adam Smith, Richard Posner, and the Philosophy of Law and Economics' (1988) 38 *University of Kansas Law Review* 209; F.I. Michelman, 'Some Uses and Abuses of Economics in Law' (1979) 46 *University of Chicago Law Review* 307.

[3] See, eg, J. Braithwaite, 'The Limits of Economism in Controlling Harmful Corporate Conduct' (1981) 16 *Law and Society Review* 481; T. Teivainen, *Enter Economism, Exit Politics: Experts, Economic Policy, and the Damage to Democracy* (New York, NY: Zed Books, 2002); G. Warren Nutter, 'On Economism' (1979) 22 *Journal of Law and Economics* 263. This is a criticism that is much broader in scope and applies to the overvaluation of economics since the advent of the neoliberal period in the late 1970s/early 1980s.

For the present purposes, however, we can make use of some of the insights that economic analysis can offer without subscribing to the political and philosophical baggage of the movement. Indeed, the concepts and tools of such analysis have by now become widely accepted across the spectrum, if only for their utility and the analytical clarity they can provide.[4] The main reason why this chapter addresses the economics of class actions is simply because economic principles and criteria are inextricable facets of aggregate litigation. From individual decision-making and lawyer's fees, costs rules and litigation funding, to policy objectives such as ensuring judicial economy and cost internalization, it is clear that the development of class actions owes a debt to the insights that economic analysis has to offer. This is particularly important from an access to justice perspective. As the Supreme Court of Canada observed in a landmark case, by allowing for the sharing of fixed litigation costs among all the class members, 'class actions improve access to justice by making economical the prosecution of claims that would otherwise be too costly to prosecute individually'.[5] Finally, class actions have also been a central pillar in classical law and economics scholarship since they often involve large economic actors like corporations and their deterrence function has implications for economic conduct on a mass scale. In this role, class actions are viewed as addressing social and economic inefficiencies created by mass unresolved justiciable problems as a result of corporate misconduct.

The global proliferation of class actions since the 1990s has also demonstrated that this economic logic is applicable elsewhere as well. The Supreme Court went on to bluntly note,

---

[4]   In the United Kingdom, see, eg, the excellent work of Jeremias and Abi Adams-Prassl, including their work that helped overturn Employment Tribunal Fees: J. Prassl and A. Adams, 'Vexatious Claims: Challenging the Case for Employment Tribunal Fees' (2017) 80(3) *Modern Law Review* 412–42.

[5]   *Western Canadian Shopping Centres Inc v Dutton* [2001] 2 SCR 534 at 28.

in that landmark case: 'Without class actions, the doors of justice remain closed to some plaintiffs, however strong their legal claims.'[6] Although this also applies to a host of social and psychological barriers – and it is paramount not to fall into the trap of economistic thinking and reduce inaccessible justice to strictly economic factors – the clearest barriers to justice that class actions contribute to overcoming are economic in nature and the economic framework is often applicable even in cases where such concerns are not the strongest factors.[7] After all, from its modern origins, the class action has involved a social dimension. The economic argument in favour of its adoption can thus be viewed as one, though certainly not the only, such argument.

Laying the groundwork

First and foremost, the main condition that must be present for a new procedure such as the class action to be a valuable addition to a procedural landscape is the existence of diffuse

---

[6]   ibid. There is also an inverse logic of this calculation that addresses the public nature of class actions and their capacity to promote social good, namely, that a vehicle that allows for the aggregation of individually non-viable claims in order to make the totality a viable claim (that is, a positive value claim) also promotes public and social goods to the extent that actual or potential wrongdoers would be deterred from engaging in wrongful conduct that results in such dispersed low-value harms.

[7]   One reason why economic argumentation is common (in favour of legal reforms, and indeed reforms in other areas as well) is because of its persuasive power, as opposed to arguments based on morality, ethics or the social good. This is perhaps indicative of the ideological primacy of economics in the current historical conjuncture and reflective of the extent to which policy and legal reform is undertaken within an economistic framework. To make such economic arguments, in this context, does not amount to an endorsement of this primacy, but is rather a pragmatic recognition of its potential in effecting socially desirable reform, such as increasing collective access to justice.

and fragmented claims. These claims do not need to be bound to a single region or geographic area, nor must they arise out of a single event. They can be distributed across vast spatial and temporal contexts. They can affect groups of individuals who have nothing in common with one another apart from their justiciable problems, groups who reside at opposite ends of a country, belong to different social and economic classes, and so forth. Consider, for instance, a faulty mass-produced product sold to consumers online, a data breach on a popular search engine or email platform, or some such cause of action. Conversely, the groups of individuals can be a cohesive collective, such as a neighbourhood or region that has experienced a toxic environmental disaster or systematic pollution, or a group of employees facing discrimination, unpaid wages or some other labour dispute on a collective basis. Whether such claims belong to a cohesive collective or simply a group of similarly situated individuals with nothing else in common does not matter: the essential point is that the claims raised have sufficient commonality so that an aggregative procedure can resolve the justiciable problem at stake to one degree or another. Finally, although not always the case, one of the distinguishing features of such claims is that they are negative value claims. The costs of pursuing them on individual bases outweigh the benefits.

Such diffuse and fragmentary claims aside, an interrelated condition is the existence of a juridical market failure. This refers to a situation whereby otherwise meritorious claims are not brought to court and individuals do not benefit from the protection of their rights provided by the law. So the absence of a procedure for aggregating such claims into a collective vehicle is a clear and obvious failure. Another market failure would be a class action regime that systematically excludes certain types of cases; for instance, cases that do not meet particular economic thresholds for enablers. In interviews conducted for this book with law firms in England and Wales, there was a broad consensus that for a class action to be viable it must conceivably meet minimum qualification criteria (for prospective damages) that were variously identified as being in the low seven-figure region.[8] This is similar to the minimum qualification criteria found in other jurisdictions. For instance, in Ontario research indicates that class action firms typically have a minimum threshold of a CAD$3–5 million for a case to be economically viable to pursue. It is thus not the case that class actions are a panacea to mass justiciable problems, but rather that they can contribute to filling collective access to justice gaps where these exist, provided that certain conditions are met to make such cases viable.

A final chief condition for introducing class actions is the existence of a structural asymmetry between claimants and defendants and the possibility of 'levelling the playing field' between the two.[9] This implicates the broader social and economic context in which mass justiciable problems arise. Generally speaking, diffuse and fragmentary harms arise out of decisions taken centrally by corporations or governments. In contrast to individual problems where the claimant and defendant are on a relatively equal footing, in the mass context the wrongdoer enjoys benefits of the economies of scale and it can invest in a defence that can be reusable against any number of claimants who must individually mount their respective cases. The structural asymmetry that is evident in this situation refers to the disadvantage experienced by claimants who have to individually bring claims against a wrongdoer who has mass-produced the wrong(s) in question.[10] In addition to the resource disparities of the respective parties which

---

[8] Respondents indicated that this figure varies depending on other contextual factors, such as the legal merits and previous experience. As a basic threshold, however, a view emerged that for a case to be worthwhile, the prospective damages must be in this region at minimum.

[9] C. Jones, *Theory of Class Actions* (Toronto: Irwin Law, 2003) at 21–7.

[10] B. Hay and D. Rosenberg, ' "Sweetheart" and "Blackmail" Settlements in Class Actions: Reality and Remedy' (2000) 75 *Notre Dame Law Review* 1383.

result in unequal litigative power, such a structural asymmetry allows the wrongdoer to invest far more into its defence than a claim is worth.[11] The implications for access to justice are profound: even where a person has a positive value claim, they can be discouraged from pursuing their claim altogether owing to this structural asymmetry, or settling for less than the claim is worth. By allowing for the aggregation of such claims into a single action, whether these claims are individually viable or non-viable, those who have suffered mass harms can level the playing field and achieve an equality of arms, and by extension rectify this structural asymmetry.[12]

In laying out the basic contours in the economics of class actions, then, we can identify the key actors as being: the class members, whose total claim value provides the foundation for the action; the lawyers, who are often the main drivers of the litigation; and a third category of actors that we will address later in this chapter, namely, the funders, who provide financial backing at the outset and over the course of the litigation, and at times provide indemnification against adverse costs awards. We can also identify the three principal goods that are achieved. The first and main good is the protection of victims and the provision of redress for those who have experienced mass harms. In economics parlance, this can be termed a 'club' good, although we can more simply refer to this as a collective good. This good is only achievable through the actions of lawyers and funders willing to take on cases, who seek private goods in the form of economic gain as a result of their respective roles in facilitating such litigation – this facet of class actions has often been highlighted by critics. Notably, however, this applies to commercial actors. For those actors who are motivated more explicitly by public interests, such

---

[11] Jones (n 9) at 22–3.

[12] No procedural innovation will totally ameliorate such asymmetries and many will continue to exist, such as informational asymmetries.

as activists, NGOs and other ideological actors, this entrepreneurial facet and the private good of economic gain would not ordinarily feature as a primary objective. Finally, there is the public good that arises from such litigation in the form of behaviour modification. By holding wrongdoers to account (and more broadly by empowering people with the capacity to hold wrongdoers to account, irrespective of whether or not this capacity is acted upon), such litigation (or the threat thereof) can have a deterrence effect with respect to other potential wrongdoers. This public good, also termed a positive externality, is a basic principle of public justice.

Enablers and incentives

At the risk of stating the obvious, in order for a class action to be brought, somebody needs to bring it. No legal action, let alone one of such magnitude, comes into being as a result of the existence of a harm, even mass harms affecting millions. The main premise of the access to justice potential that animates class actions – that individuals are not incentivized to bring their own claims by virtue of the claims being individually non-viable – indicates that some actor needs to be incentivized to bring the claim on behalf of a group of such individuals. This incentive can be organic to the bringer of the claim, as in the case of ideological actors or organizations who are motivated not by economic gain (or at least not primarily by such private gain) but rather by the promotion of collective and public goods. Typically, however, the main actor who needs to be incentivized to bring the claim is the class action lawyer (or increasingly a third party funder) who does so based primarily on the prospect of private economic gain.[13] In theory, of course, it is not only the lawyers or funders who

---

[13] For a good overview of the economic incentives of class actions, see J.G. Backhaus, A. Cassone and B. Ramello, *The Law and Economics of Class Actions in Europe* (Cheltenham: Edward Elgar, 2012); M. Hvid

can act as economic enablers of actions, but also those who have incurred the harms being litigated. We can thus begin by setting out the framework of claimants as enablers, before moving on to the other key actors.

Claimants as enablers

The standard economic argument about the access to justice benefits of opt-out class actions is relatively straightforward and rooted in the rational choice framework of orthodox economics. It can be briefly summarized as follows: many collective harms involve a large number of victims who have incurred harms of relatively modest value. These justiciable problems, if they were to be taken forward as legal disputes, can be called negative value claims, which refers to claims where the projected costs of litigation outweigh the projected value of the claim. No rational actor would bring forth such a claim as they are individually unviable. This holds true across all justiciable problems, not just those involving collective harms, as those with negative value claims are systematically excluded from formal legal avenues of dispute resolution. Although other fora of dispute resolution, apart from courts, may have lower costs and barriers to entry, the formal logic of the rational economic actor with a negative value claim applies in those contexts as well: where costs outweigh benefits, a rational actor will not pursue a claim, irrespective of its merits.[14]

---

and J. Peysner, 'Comparing Economic Incentives to Pursue Private Actions across EU Member States' in B. Rodger (ed), *Competition Law: Comparative Private Enforcement and Collective Redress Across the EU* (Alphen aan den Rijn: Kluwer Law International, 2014). This chapter especially owes a debt to C. Cameron, J. Kalajdzic and A. Klement, 'Economic Enablers' in D.R. Hensler, C. Hodges and I. Tzankova (eds), *Class Actions in Context: How Culture, Economics and Politics Shape Collective Litigation* (Cheltenham: Edward Elgar, 2016) at 137–69.

[14] A disclaimer of sorts is also needed. When speaking of the access to justice potential of aggregating individually non-viable claims and these

The decision of such an actor not to pursue a meritorious case can be described as a problem of rational disinterest or rational apathy that results in a social loss and market failure given the negative externality it produces (a cost is incurred in society for which the wrongdoer is not held liable). Where collective justiciable problems are involved and class actions are available, however, the situation changes: if there is a sufficient number of people with the same or similar claims against one (or several) wrongdoers, then aggregating these claims can make it a viable case to pursue. This occurs when the costs and risks of litigation are shared between the members of the class.[15] Simply put, where a sufficient number of negative value claims are aggregated to the point where the totality becomes of positive value, a case becomes viable to litigate as costs no longer outweigh benefits. By facilitating such actions, a regime also addresses the social loss and market failure produced by rational apathy as society no longer suffers from the negative externality of the harm and wrongdoers must internalize the costs of their wrongdoing.

It is rare for a claimant to be the chief enabler of a class action for the reasons identified earlier. The relatively low value of the claims involved in most class actions means that

---

being economically irrational to pursue on individual bases, this must not be interpreted as somehow discounting the possibility of claims being pursued by 'economically irrational actors', nor indeed delegitimizing such actors. While the term 'irrational' has obvious negative cultural connotations, in this context it simply refers to the individual decision making in the context of pursuing litigation and is not deployed in an aspersive manner. Any number of cases of public importance have been pursued based on principle rather than economics – when a person seeks to address a wrong done unto them as a matter of principle, irrespective of the costs involved; where the impetus for the recourse to the law is morality, ethics or the social good, as opposed to any economic benefits that the claim may yield for the claimant.

[15] These can also be shared with other key actors, such as lawyers and funders.

no individual has the incentive necessary to bring the claim. If an individual does not have the incentive to bring a claim on their own behalf – and are rationally apathetic – they do not have the incentive to bring a claim on behalf of others, most if not all of whom they do not (and will never) know. This applies to all class members. Even in cases where an individual may have a higher claim value, the incentive still may not be sufficient to bring the claim on behalf of a group, given the so-called free rider problem, another market failure, whereby individuals prefer to gain from the benefits that the litigation can yield (off the back of the work of others, so to speak), without putting in the work of actively bringing the claim and exposing themselves to the associated costs and risks in the process. Additionally, the real value of a claim is not always discernible by victims. In cases of data violations, for example, there are serious difficulties in quantifying the harm incurred by the victims and, by extension, the value of their claims and the compensation owed to them.

For most class action regimes, however, there must be a representative claimant who, at least formally, is understood to bring the claim on behalf of the class. In some regimes, this representative claimant has to assume the risks of adverse costs. If bringing such a claim on one's own behalf were an economically irrational thing to do, bringing it on behalf of a group of people and assuming the risks of paying the defendant's costs upon losing in court makes it a practically inconceivable act for a rational person.[16] In addition to acting as the class

---

[16] This reflects what the Ontario Superior Court of Justice called the 'grim reality' of class actions, particularly in regimes with a loser pays rule. 'No person in their right mind,' Justice Strathy observed, 'would accept the role of representative plaintiff if he or she were at risk of losing everything they own. No one, no matter how altruistic, would risk such a loss over a modest claim. Indeed, no rational person would risk an adverse costs award of several million dollars to recover several thousand dollars or even several tens of thousand dollars.' *Dugal v Manulife Financial Corporation* [2011] ONSC 1785 at 29.

representative in court, this individual is often tasked with monitoring the conduct of the class lawyer to ensure the best interests of the class. If an individual does not have the incentive to bring the claim, either on behalf of themselves or on behalf of the group, they can scarcely be viewed as having the incentive necessary to monitor the lawyer.

This situation gives rise to a standard principal–agent problem. Such a problem occurs when an actor (the agent) is entrusted to act on behalf of another actor (the principal). In the context of class actions, the agent is the lawyer and the principal is the class, with the representative claimant being a constituent member of the principal. The problem occurs when the principal, or in this case a representative of the principal, does not (or cannot) properly monitor the agent to ensure that the agent is actually acting in the best interests of the principal, which creates the risk that the agent can act in its own best interest. In other words, the representative class member often does not have the capacity to adequately monitor the class lawyer – a situation that may lead the class lawyer to act in its own best interest rather than in the interests of the class, or at any rate, a situation that creates the risk of this type of conduct. That representative claimants are often recruited by the lawyer in practice gives reason for pause for those concerned with this principal–agent problem. This is why the representative claimant is often viewed as a something of a fiction erected to maintain the illusion that the client is in charge. A radical solution to this would be to remove the requirement for such a representative altogether and scrutinize the lawyer (or funder), to embrace these actors as the drivers of litigation and to subject them accordingly to enhanced scrutiny. Similar concerns have been raised elsewhere, leading to various reforms to address the reality that the representative claimant often has neither the economic interest nor the capacity to monitor the lawyer.[17]

---

[17] As Alon Klement has observed, 'representative plaintiffs have proven to be merely figureheads: ineffective, passive, unsophisticated, and completely

A less radical solution to this problem is to take a more flexible approach to the requirement of a representative claimant. Instead of requiring that the representative has to be a member of the class – that is, a person who has incurred the harm that has given rise to the litigation – some regimes, such as in England and Wales, have taken the progressive step to allow ideological claimants to act as representatives of the class. This refers to typically public-oriented actors such as NGOs, consumer protection groups, environmental organizations, labour unions, human rights groups and the like, who have an interest in the substantive content of the litigation, but do not have a direct interest in the form of having incurred a harm. In order to ensure wide accessibility, such an approach should not foreclose the possibility of a representative of the class bringing the claim, nor should it be restricted to pre-identified

---

disregarded by both courts and class attorneys', A. Klement, 'Who Should Guard the Guardians? A New Approach for Monitoring Class Action Lawyers' (2002) 21 *Review of Litigation* 27–8. The literature on representative claimants is understandably large, given its centrality as one of the chief points of criticism. See, eg, J.E. Fisch, 'Class Action Reform, "Qui Tam", and the Role of the Plaintiff' (1997) 60(4) *Law and Contemporary Problems* 167–202; J.R. Macey and G.P. Miller, 'The Plaintiffs' Attorney's Role in Class Action and Derivative Litigation: Economic Analysis and Recommendations for Reform' (1991) 58(1) *The University of Chicago Law Review* 1–118; J.C. Coffee, 'Class Action Wars: The Dilemma of the Mass Tort Class Action' (1995) 95(6) *Columbia Law Review* 1343–465; K.W. Dam, 'Class Actions: Efficiency, Compensation, Deterrence, and Conflict of Interest' (1975) 4(1) *The Journal of Legal Studies* 47–73; E.J. Weiss and J.S. Beckerman, 'Let the Money Do the Monitoring: How Institutional Investors Can Reduce Agency Costs in Securities Class Actions' (1995) 104(8) *Yale Law Journal* 2053–127; J.W. Welch, 'Continuation and Representation of Class Actions Following Dismissal of the Class Representative' (1974) 3 *Duke Law Journal* 573–609; J.D. Cox, R.S. Thomas and D. Kiku, 'Does the Plaintiff Matter? An Empirical Analysis of Lead Plaintiffs in Securities Class Actions' (2006) 106(7) *Columbia Law Review* 1587–640; J.C. Coffee, 'Litigation Governance: Taking Accountability Seriously' (2010) 110(2) *Columbia Law Review* 288–351.

organizations but should rather be open to any organization that can meet the requirements of representation (for example that can demonstrate that it can fulfil its duties to the class). The standing rules that determine who may bring actions as representatives – claimants, ideological claimants or both – have often been a matter of strong dispute in reform processes, with the growing recognition in England and Wales that allowing for a wide range of actors (both types of claimants) is preferable from an accessibility perspective.

Lawyers as enablers

There is scarcely a facet of class actions that has been so intensely analysed as the class action lawyer, whose role in facilitating litigation has been variously viewed as both a social good and a social evil. The various conceptualizations of the class action lawyer offer insights into why this is the case. For those who view class action lawyers in a positive light, as social advocates or at the very least as actors pursuing social goods, the term 'private attorney general' is sometimes invoked. This is a term used to describe a private legal actor who pursues social goods for private economic gain. It rose to prominence with the Second Wave of the movement in the late 1960s and early 1970s, quickly becoming an 'accepted character' in the United States and a widely supported 'legal institution'.[18] As Owen Fiss has observed, the figure of the private attorney general is the combination of 'two different agencies: public officers and private citizens'.[19] Bryant Garth et al have also observed that

---

[18] B. Garth, I.H. Nagel and S.J. Plager, 'The Institution of the Private Attorney General: Perspectives from an Empirical Study of Class Action Litigation' (1988) 61 *Southern California Law Review* 352. See also C. Cheng, 'Important Rights and the Private Attorney General Doctrine' (1985) 73(6) *California Law Review* 1929.

[19] O. Fiss, 'The Political Theory of the Class Action' (1996) 53(1) *Washington and Lee Law Review* 21.

the private attorney general can be viewed as a 'mercenary law enforcer' or 'bounty hunter' whose entrepreneurial character drives case selection, while at the same time acting as a 'social advocate' who pursues mass claims to ensure victims receive compensation and deterrence is promoted where public authorities are recalcitrant or unable to undertake enforcement.[20] The basic idea that animates this conceptualization of the class action lawyer is that there is a public-oriented role to play for private actors in pursuing enforcement, a role that is made possible with the right economic incentives in place. This last point is worth emphasizing. Even in such a relatively positive conceptualization, there is never any illusion that such a lawyer is acting out of altruism or solely for the public good. Far from being removed from the discussion, the economic reality of litigation – the conditions, incentives and rules that facilitate litigation – must be incorporated into the design of class action regimes in order to promote greater access to justice, deterrence and judicial economy, starting with those features that govern the conduct of lawyers.[21]

The same economies of scale that must be present for a class action to be a viable solution for addressing mass wrongs (at the level of civil justice design and reform) must also be present for such cases to be viable for lawyers to pursue. Class actions are complex forms of litigation, involving significant investments of resources. Expenditures include disbursements, such as expert testimony, commissioned studies, evidence formation, and private investigation. Lawyers must also invest a considerable amount of time in bringing such cases, including often prolonged periods in pre-trial motions and procedures, depending on the regime. The capital-intensive nature of such cases means that the expected returns for the

---

[20] Garth et al (n 18) at 356.

[21] Critics, conversely, have sought to portray such lawyers as bounty hunters whose entrepreneurialism distorts the proper administration of justice.

lawyer must be significant enough to cover such expenditures, including opportunity costs and risks of adverse costs awards (in jurisdictions like England and Wales that enforce the 'loser pays' rule).

A prime method that system designers have deployed to incentivize lawyers to bring class actions forward has been to allow for contingency fees. In order for a lawyer to be incentivized to bring an action, in an entrepreneurial capacity, there must be some form of contingency fee available (also known in the United Kingdom as a damages-based agreement). At its simplest, this refers to a percentage of the total recovery, typically taken out of a 'common fund', and is a fee that the lawyer receives only upon success. Where the action does not result in victory at trial or a settlement, the lawyer does not receive any remuneration. For a contingency fee regime to be effective in making the lawyer an enabler of actions, then, it must account for this risk (and the opportunity costs) and cannot simply be designed to cover the costs that the lawyer has incurred. To properly enable lawyers to pursue such litigation, a contingency fee regime must reward lawyers more than the value of their inputted resources.[22]

Somewhat predictably, one outcome of such fees has been an increasing focus on high-value claims (all else being equal), which has usually meant shareholder and securities actions, as opposed to lower-value claims that may be of greater public importance, such as human rights violations or environmental harms.[23] In 2012, in public consultations on reform for private

---

[22] There are different types of contingency fees and methods by which lawyers' fees can be calculated, including the standard flat rate or percentage of recovery, as well as multipliers and what is called the lodestar method in the United States, which is the calculation of the product of reasonable hours inputted at a reasonable hourly rate, with a number of other variants (eg lodestar multiplier).

[23] Of course, shareholder and securities claims have some public importance, not least because of their deterrence and private regulatory function.

actions in competition law, UK lawmakers signalled an alertness to this possibility and the potential for such incentives to result in this kind of prioritization. This resulted in a prohibition on contingency fees. 'The Government agrees that this prohibition would be an important safeguard and that allowing DBAs [Damages Based Agreements] could encourage speculative litigation,' the official response noted, 'thereby placing unjustified costs on defendant businesses and creating an incentive for lawyers to focus only on the largest cases.'[24]

This reflects a recognition that the class action lawyer is a gatekeeper of sorts and speaks to a central dynamic in class action litigation: the reversal of the traditional recruitment paradigm. Whereas in most types of litigation, the client recruits the lawyer, in class actions it is generally the case that the lawyer recruits the client. This is why the representative claimant is often viewed as a fiction or a figurehead. There is a long-standing history and judicial acceptance of such recruitment, especially in test cases involving civil rights litigation, but such recruitment by entrepreneurial lawyers for economic gain has not been given the same warm reception.

In such a dynamic, the conditions of recruitment can take on the characteristics of barriers. There are, however, two sides to this coin. On one side, this dynamic can be viewed as limiting access to justice for those with claims that do not meet the minimum qualification criteria at case selection. On the other, this dynamic can be viewed as promoting access to justice, particularly in cases where victims may not be aware (or may be otherwise ignorant) of the fact that they have been victimized, or where victims may lack the legal consciousness, empowerment or capacity to pursue their claims. In such

---

[24] Department for Business, Innovation & Skills, *Private Actions in Competition Law: A Consultation on Options for Reform – Government Response*, January 2013 at 5.62. Notably, no win, no fee conditional agreements and after-the-event insurance were not deemed to encourage such speculative litigation and were accepted as such.

situations, a lawyer alerting victims of the harms they have incurred and providing the legal services that they otherwise would not have received can result in a mutually beneficial outcome for both actors. That a case is selected by a lawyer based on economic motivations does not mean that it does not also have public importance and cannot also promote access to justice for groups of people who have suffered harms. For designers of regimes, however, it is important that the economic incentives of the lawyer remain aligned with those of the class, so that situations do not occur where a lawyer is tempted to settle early, for less than the claim is worth, or engage in other misconduct that disadvantages the class.[25] This is why proper safeguards and monitoring need to be in place to ensure optimality of outcomes.

For jurisdictions that have sought to introduce class actions as legal transplants, this entrepreneurial role of the lawyer in driving the litigation – from identifying potential mass wrongs to recruiting a representative and taking the case forward – has been a primary cause for concern. Entrepreneurial litigation, as such, has been viewed as a distinctly American phenomenon, and reformers elsewhere, including in England and Wales, have expressly sought to avoid the excesses that are associated with 'US-style class actions'. Although such arguments are often neither empirically sound nor comparatively viable – in England and Wales, for instance, there are no punitive damages, no contingency fees and no civil juries, thus rendering such fears of importing 'American litigation culture' unfounded – the idea of incentivizing lawyers to act as enablers is not uncontroversial. Typically, resistance to lawyers as enablers is grounded not only in differing legal cultures – a decidedly amorphous concept that lends itself to abuse – but also in doctrinal considerations, most obviously the doctrines of maintenance and champerty,

---

[25] This is particularly important as the class is typically absent from the proceedings, with the exception of the class representative.

which seek to restrict or prevent such entrepreneurial legal activity. As the growing role of commercial funders in this space attests, these doctrines have come under increasing scrutiny and have, to varying extents, been repealed to allow for such economic enablers to take effect.

Private funders as enablers

The traditional view of the lawyer as the key enabler who needs to be sufficiently incentivized to take on the costs and risks of bringing an action has been nuanced in recent years with the emergence of third party litigation funding. This typically refers to commercial funders who assume the costs (and often the risks) of litigation, in exchange for a share of the proceeds.[26] Concurrent with the global expansion of class

---

[26] I have written elsewhere about the emergence of the litigation finance industry in the context of class actions. See M. Molavi, 'Law's Financialisation: Litigation Finance and Multilayer Access to Justice in Canada' (2019) 33(3) *Canadian Journal of Law and Society / Revue Canadienne Droit et Société* 425–45. See also, E.C. Burch, 'Financiers as Monitors in Aggregate Litigation' (2012) 87 *New York University Law Review* 1273–338; C. Cameron and J. Kalajdzic, 'Commercial Litigation Funding: Ethical, Regulatory and Comparative Perspectives' (2014) 55(1) *Canadian Business Law Journal* 1–16; M. De Morpurgo, 'A Comparative Legal and Economic Approach to Third-Party Litigation Funding' (2011) 19 *Cardozo Journal of International and Comparative Law* 343–412; C. Hodges, J. Peynser and A. Nurse, 'Litigation Funding: Status and Issues', *Oxford Legal Studies Research Paper* No. 55, available at https://ssrn.com/abstract=2126506; J. Kalajdzic, P. Cashman and A. Longmoore, 'Justice for Profit: A Comparative Analysis of Australian, Canadian and US Third Party Litigation Funding' (2013) 61(2) *American Journal of Comparative Law* 93–148; P. Puri, 'Financing of Litigation by Third-Party Investors: A Share of Justice?' (1998) 36(3) *Osgoode Hall Law Journal* 515–66; A. Sebok, 'Litigation Investment and Legal Ethics: What Are the Real Issues?' (2014) 55 *Canadian Business Law Journal* 111–32; P. Senkpiel, 'Three's a Crowd: Third Party Litigation Funding of Class Actions in Canada' (2009) 5(2) *Canadian Class Action Review* 294–329; M. Steinitz, 'Whose Claim Is It Anyway? Third Party Litigation Funding' (2011)

actions, third party litigation funding has also proliferated in recent years[27] in response to the high costs and risks associated with litigation more broadly, and mass litigation specifically.[28]

The interplay of rules governing costs and fees determines the extent of the role played by third party funders. In England and Wales, where contingency fees are not permitted for class action lawyers, it is not surprising that litigation funders have taken an active role (all class actions in the Competition Appeal Tribunal have thus far been externally funded). The most reputable funders in this jurisdiction are members of the Association of Litigation Funders, an independent body charged by the Ministry of Justice with regulating the industry.[29] They abide by a Code of Conduct, published by the Civil Justice Council in 2011, which sets out the standards to which funders must adhere, including ensuring capital adequacy and preventing funders from exercising control over litigation or settlement negotiations. In his Review of Civil Litigation Costs in 2009, Lord Justice Jackson recognized that an approach like the current Code of Conduct that regulates the industry was a

---

95(4) *Minnesota Law Review* 1268–338; M. Trebilcock and E. Kagedan, 'An Economic Assessment of Third-Party Litigation Funding' (2014) 55(1) *Canadian Business Law Journal* 54–84; S. Yeazell, 'Refinancing Civil Litigation' (2001) 51 *DePaul Law Review* 183–217.

[27] Other desirable conditions are also present that account for the growth of third party litigation funding from the perspective of funders, such as the relatively insulated market of courtrooms, that litigation investments are uncorrelated zero-beta assets and the like. See Molavi (n 26) at 1.

[28] Several jurisdictions have permitted some form of litigation financing in recent years in addition to England and Wales, including Australia, Austria, Brazil, Cayman Islands, Denmark, Germany, Hong Kong, Ireland, South Korea, the Netherlands, New Zealand, Poland, Singapore, Switzerland and the United States.

[29] Members of the Association of Litigation Funders in England and Wales include Augusta Ventures Ltd, Balance Legal Capital LLP, Burford Capital, Calunius Capital LLP, Harbour Litigation Funding Ltd, Redress Solutions PLC, Therium Capital Management Ltd, Vannin Capital PCC and Woodsford Litigation Funding Ltd.

preferable, given the industry's nascency, with the potential for further regulatory oversight to be determined at a later date, pending its growth. Whether the time has come to revisit the regulatory approach taken thus far remains an open question.[30]

Lord Justice Jackson also offered strong support for third party funding, noting that it provides funding for litigation where this may not be available and thus promotes access to justice. 'It is now recognised that many claimants cannot afford to pursue valid claims without third party funding,' he observed, and 'that it is better for such claimants to forfeit a percentage of their damages than to recover nothing at all.'[31] In interviews with funders undertaken for this book, there was a saturation point achieved that a prospective claim needs to meet a minimum monetary threshold to be viable to pursue – similar to the conditions imposed by class lawyers in other jurisdictions; this was said to be £3–6 million, while some noted that the complexity of the claim and the risks involved could increase this minimum. Funders also noted that their expected returns on investment were relatively high on paper (most observed expected returns between two and four times their investment or between 15 and 40 per cent of the recovery in addition to the full return of the investment) but this accounted for the unpredictability of litigation and the nascency of the industry. Funders also noted that the expected ratio between expected

---

[30] There was no hostility towards new regulation by interviewed funders, with many underscoring that such regulation must be aimed at ensuring the proper administration of justice and should not be intended (as the Institute for Legal Reform has suggested) as a way to unduly prevent funding for either high-value commercial cases, aggregated litigation and class actions, or other types of fundable claims. Giving state enforcement capacities to the Association of Litigation Funders' self-regulatory Code of Conduct was viewed by many as a reasonable step forward, if such regulation was desired by government.

[31] Lord Justice Jackson, *Review of Civil Litigation Costs: Final Report* at 117.

damages and expected outlay was typically 10:1. As one senior executive wryly relayed,

> 'I've heard the term *elephant hunter* being bandied about and I think that's unfair. We're not interested in lower values, relatively speaking, that's true, but litigation funding wouldn't exist if there wasn't a need and it's only natural for us to do our due diligence and make sure we're investing wisely to protect our investment.'[32]

Far from promoting frivolous or vexatious litigation, the selection criteria of third party funders can act as a filtering process since there is no incentive to advance unmeritorious claims that would fail to yield returns. Lord Justice Jackson echoed this view: 'Third party funding tends to filter out unmeritorious cases, because funders will not take on the risk of such cases. This benefits opposing parties.'[33] The role of litigation funders as the main economic enablers is similar in Australia, where the third party funding industry has taken the strongest hold globally, and contrasts with the situation in the United States, where lawyers continue to be the main economic enablers. This reflects rules governing fees in the respective jurisdictions.

Costs rules are also important factors in determining whether or not there is a market need for third party funders. Where the loser pays principle is applied, funders can provide indemnification against any adverse costs awards instead of, or in addition to, providing funding.[34] This need is clearly obviated where each side bears its own costs, as in the United States. Looking at the situation in England and Wales, with its rejection of contingency fees and adverse cost-shifting rules (and

---

[32] Respondent 13, interviewed on 7 December 2018.
[33] Lord Justice Jackson (n 31) at 117.
[34] In Ontario, for example, this is the main market gap that litigation funders contribute to filling.

the absence of a public funder, addressed later), it is clear that funders will play an important role in promoting collective access to justice by enabling class actions.

The emergence of third party funding since the late 2000s has garnered a lot of controversy, unsurprisingly. There is a noticeable overlap in the legal and political criticisms of both class actions and third party funding and it is understandable why this is the case: both class actions and third party funders give rise to concerns about the role market forces can play in the administration of justice and the uneasy relationship that may exist between economic and legal principles. These concerns are often based, in their modern invocation, on the desire to avoid abusive or frivolous litigation. Available evidence suggests, however, that far from promoting unmeritorious litigation, third party funders act as gatekeepers and devote significant time to monitoring and screening prospective claims in which they invest – the idea that such funders would promote unmeritorious claims is not borne out by either economic theory or practice.[35] The incentive of funders is to pursue strong meritorious claims that will result in attractive rewards on investments. From an access to justice perspective, many of the same concerns about the prioritization of certain types of cases to the exclusion of others (that may have greater public importance) apply to third party funding as well. The reality remains that as promising as such enabling may be, where the value of a claim is small, it will not elicit interest from funders, irrespective of the merits.

The main doctrinal objections to third party funding, based on the doctrines of maintenance and champerty, have similarly been invoked against class actions, most notably in the debate over the legitimacy of contingency fees. Maintenance can be

---

[35] See, eg, W.H. Van Boom, 'Litigation Costs and Third-Party Funding' in W.H. Van Boom (ed), *Litigation, Costs, Funding and Behaviour: Implication for the Law* (London: Routledge, 2017) at 5–30.

understood as occurring when an actor encourages the pursuit of a lawsuit in which that actor does not have a proper or legitimate interest; it applies in cases where a disinterested third party enables a legal action.[36] Champerty refers to a variant of maintenance in which the actor has a financial stake in the litigation and stands to profit from it.[37] Without the former, the latter does not exist. The origins of these doctrines have not been decisively traced,[38] although the earliest formulations found thus far are from medieval England, with champerty finding its long-lasting expression in the 1305 Statutum de Conspiratoribus (Statute Concerning Conspirators). It is

---

[36] Maintenance was defined well by Fletcher Moulton LJ in *British Cash and Parcel Conveyors v Lamson Store Service Company* [1908] 1 KB 1006 at 1014: 'It is directed against wanton and officious intermeddling with the disputes of others in which the [maintainer] has no interest whatever, and where the assistance he renders to one or the other party is without justification or excuse.' See also, *Giles v Thompson* [1994] 1 AC 142, [1993] UKHL 2, [1993] 3 All ER 321, [1994] AC 42.

[37] Although maintenance and champerty are the two main doctrinal objections, another relevant doctrine is that of barratry, which simply refers to the stirring of vexatious litigation.

[38] Lord Mustill has offered a succinct overview of both doctrines as follows:

> The crimes of maintenance and champerty are so old that their origins can no longer be traced, but their importance in medieval times is quite clear. The mechanisms of justice lacked the internal strength to resist the oppression of private individuals through suits fomented and sustained by unscrupulous men of power. Champerty was particularly vicious, since the purchase of a share in litigation presented an obvious temptation to the suborning of justices and witnesses and the exploitation of worthless claims which the defendant lacked the resources and influence to withstand. The fact that such conduct was treated as both criminal and tortious provided an invaluable external discipline to which, as the records show, recourse was often required.

Giles v Thompson at 1.

important to note that the original objectives of both doctrines were not only to avoid vexatious or frivolous litigation, but to prevent litigation altogether, irrespective of the merits. From the late 19th century onwards, however, attitudes began to shift and the two doctrines were progressively liberalized to allow for exemptions with a view towards balancing the objectives of promoting access to justice while also continuing to discourage frivolous or vexatious litigation.[39] Both doctrines stopped being criminal law offences with the passing of the Criminal Law Act 1967.[40] There have, of course, been exceptions carved out to the doctrines over the years, such as those recommended in the 1945 Rushcliffe Report, with the introduction of legal aid and the growth of litigation funded by trade unions, as the Law Commission observed in 1967 (recommending the abolition of both doctrines).[41] In light of the recent retrenchment of access to justice in England and Wales, most notably the passage of the Legal Aid, Sentencing and Punishment of Offenders Act 2012 (LASPO) and broader cuts to public provisioning, the desirability of private financing as a potential complement to (or substitute for) public legal aid has contributed to the curtailment of both doctrines.[42]

The rise of third party funding has elicited a forceful lobbying and public campaign by the US Chamber of Commerce's Institute for Legal Reform and Justice Not Profit, which has taken direct aim at both class actions and third party funding in

---

[39] Molavi (n 26) at 10.

[40] Criminal Law Act 1967, s 14(1).

[41] Lord Neuberger, 'From Barratry, Maintenance and Champerty to Litigation Funding' (Harbour Litigation Funding First Annual Lecture, Gray's Inn, 8 May 2013) at para 37.

[42] J. Peysner, 'Expropriation, Access to Justice (and Wikileaks): A Comparative Study of Funding Difficult Cases in England and Wales and the United States' (2013) 31(1) *Civil Justice Quarterly* 1–14. Although these doctrines have been repealed, the concerns that gave rise to them, namely, the avoidance of vexatious or frivolous litigation, remain for policymakers.

the United Kingdom (recognizing the importance of the latter to the former) by raising alarms that allowing such funding would amount to allowing financial speculators to manipulate the justice system for profit by peddling vexatious litigation.[43] The Institute for Legal Reform has advocated for a robust oversight regime and strict regulation of the industry. According to this lobby, the potential risks of third party funding 'are simply too acute to be left to industry self-regulation'.[44] Presumably the acuteness of these risks is worse than that in other areas for which the Chamber of Commerce has waged deregulatory (and anti-regulatory) campaigns, including against environmental, financial, healthcare, employment and consumer protection.[45] Among the lobbying objectives has tellingly been an outright ban on the use of such funding 'in relation to class actions of all kinds'.[46]

Meanwhile, proponents have embraced this development as a promising change in the right direction provided that safeguards are in place to protect the interests of class members and the administration of justice. For instance, in 2013, Lord Neuberger identified that 'funding was the life-blood of the

---

[43] Justice Not Profit, 'Key Asks: Third Party Litigation Funding', available at https://www.justicenotprofit.co.uk/key-asks/. J.H. Beisner and G.A. Rubin, US Chamber of Commerce Institute for Legal Reform, 'Stopping the Sale of Lawsuits: A Proposal to Regulate Third-Party Investments in Litigation' (2012). See also J.H. Beisner, US Chamber of Commerce Institute for Legal Reform, 'Buying Lawsuits, Selling Trouble: Third-Party Litigation Funding in the United States' (2009).

[44] Beisner and Rubin (n 43) at 7.

[45] As William Wendel has observed, an 'objection to the commodification of civil justice is likely to be purely strategic unless it is part of a broader theoretical agenda that seeks to displace economic modes of valuation from areas of life in which they do not belong', W. Wendel, 'Alternative Litigation Finance and Anti-Commodification Norms' (2014) 63(2) DePaul Law Review 659.

[46] Other objectives include that all funders should be subject to full adverse costs, and the funders should be prevented from withdrawing from funded litigation. See Justice Not Profit (n 43).

justice system' and that the growth of the industry has signalled a positive shift in public policy.[47] This perspective had been echoed centuries before by Jeremy Bentham, who referred to the prohibitions against litigation funding as 'barbarous precaution[s]' from a 'barbarous age', and who took the view that the vast majority of people were effectively denied justice with the prohibitions in place, their impact being to give wealth a 'monopoly of justice against poverty'.[48] As Lord Neuberger observed, paraphrasing Bentham's critique, 'as long as litigation, access to the courts, remains expensive, then anyone who has a right that stands in need of vindication should be able to obtain funding from anyone willing to offer it and on whatever terms it is offered'.[49] This is based on the view that 'access to the courts is a right, and the state should not stand in the way of individuals availing themselves of that right'.[50] We could perhaps go further: not only should the state not stand in the way of individuals in such a manner, there is even a proactive role for the state to play in funding collective access to justice, even in the post-LASPO, post-Jackson reforms period of squeezing fiscal space, as the following models demonstrate.

Public funders as enablers

Although third party funders for class actions are usually commercial actors, that is not always the case. Public funders can be extremely valuable additions to the funding options available for prospective claimants. Such public funders can fill a market gap by supporting cases of greater public importance that would not otherwise be appealing for commercial actors

---

[47] Lord Neuberger (n 41) at para 52.
[48] ibid at paras 26, 33.
[49] ibid at para 46.
[50] ibid.

seeking profit maximization.[51] Indeed, public funders are often required by statute to take on cases with public interests at stake. In many other ways, however, public funders are similar to commercial funders. They likewise consider the economic viability of cases and engage in what would have historically been called 'champertous behaviour' by investing in cases and receiving a share of the proceeds (if successful; and in unsuccessful cases they are often liable for adverse costs where the loser pays principle applies) – and by extension, of course, they are incentivized to pursue meritorious cases that have a high likelihood of success. While the very idea of a public funder might seem, at first glance, to fly in the face of the budgetary retrenchment of access to justice, successful examples of such funders illustrate why this model is feasible, even in the current period of limited state expenditures.

The two leading examples of public funding can be found in the Canadian provinces of Ontario and Quebec. In the former, the Ontario Class Proceedings Fund was established in 1993 alongside Ontario's class action legislation in recognition of the significant problems of financing class actions faced by claimants. It was initially established with a $500,000 endowment from the Law Foundation of Ontario, with funding coverage of adverse costs awards and disbursements. With this seed money in place, the Class Proceedings Fund was tasked with considering several factors before funding prospective actions, including both the public interest and the strength of the claim. As the Fund was created to advance the objectives of the legislation, each of the cases it has funded has promoted collective access to justice, as the primary objective, as well

---

[51] This does not suggest, in any way, that commercial funders do not take on cases with public importance, and there are plenty of examples of commercially funded public interest cases, but rather that such considerations are not primary in their decision-making (nor for that matter is it reasonable to expect that they should be – these are, after all, profit-driven enterprises).

as advancing one or more public interests. Many cases have also resulted in the establishment of new legal principles and the development of jurisprudence. Far from being a burden on the public purse, the Fund operates on a financially self-sustaining model. It imposes a 10 per cent levy of any awards or settlements in favour of claimants in funded proceedings, in addition to the return of any funded disbursements. This self-sustaining model has been extremely successful: by the time of its 20-year review in 2012, the Fund had grown to a stable financial position of roughly $24 million. Despite a few high-profile cases of unsuccessful actions, resulting in significant losses, levies for the Fund continue to rise at higher rates than costs and it remains in strong financial health.

Collective access to justice has been promoted by the Fund in a wide range of cases that would likely not otherwise have been pursued due to a lack of financing and risk exposures, covering a wide range of claims including those arising out of pension mismanagement,[52] unjust enrichment involving live events and Ticketmaster,[53] misconduct by higher education institutions,[54] usurious loans to vulnerable people,[55] credit card charges,[56] environmental pollution,[57] copyright infringement,[58] regulatory negligence on the part of Health Canada,[59] unpaid overtime wages,[60] long-term

---

[52] These and a number of other cases funded by the Class Proceedings Fund were highlighted in its 20-year review report. See, eg, *Givogue v Burke* in Class Proceedings Fund, *Class Proceedings Fund: 20 Years in Review* (2012) at 5.

[53] *Krajewski v Ticketmaster* in ibid at 6.

[54] See, eg, *Hickey-Button and Potter v Loyalist College* in ibid at 5.

[55] *Smith v Money Mart, Mortillaro v Cash Money* and *Mortillaro v Unicash* in ibid at 7.

[56] *Gilbert v CIBC, Meretsky v BNS, Cassano v TD Bank* in ibid at 7.

[57] *Hollick v The City of Metropolitan Toronto* in ibid at 8.

[58] *Robertson v Thomson* in ibid at 9.

[59] *Taylor v Canada (Attorney General)* in ibid at 9.

[60] *McCracken v Canadian National Railway* in ibid at 10.

disability,[61] rent reductions for low-income housing,[62] medical product liability,[63] unlawful arrests at the G20 protests in Toronto in 2010,[64] and the abuse of Indigenous children in residential facilities.[65] The importance of a generic opt-out class action regime and the need for private enforcement is on display in this representative sample of cases supported by the Fund. Those who have suffered from justiciable problems in these cases have typically been vulnerable people without recourse to justice but for the existence of class actions. It is likewise important to observe that such cases have not only been advanced against powerful corporate entities, such as Ticketmaster, Pfizer, CIBC, TD Bank and Money Mart, but also against state bodies and agencies, including the City of Toronto, Health Canada and the Toronto Police Services Board.

Despite the relative strength of Ontario's Class Proceedings Fund, a potential reform that jurisdictions like England and Wales may consider is to modify its fixed 10 per cent levy to encourage greater flexibility and promote applications that have otherwise been disincentivized. There are cases, for example, that have more reasonable prospects of success and may thus warrant lower levies. That its funding is only available for disbursements and adverse costs awards can also be a matter open to reform, as it does not cover lawyers' fees. These features have likely contributed to the relatively low usage rate of the Class Proceedings Fund (10–20 per cent of proceedings in Ontario). By way of contrast, the funding model found in Quebec, Fonds d'aide aux recours collectifs, also offers funding

---

[61] *Ruffolo v Sun Life* in ibid at 10.

[62] *Williams v City of Toronto* in ibid at 10.

[63] *Crisante v Slotec, Parker v Pfizer, Shick v Boehringer* in ibid at 11.

[64] *Good v Toronto Police Services Board* in ibid at 11.

[65] *Bechard v Her Majesty the Queen, Dolmage v Her Majesty the Queen, Seed v Her Majesty the Queen* in ibid at 11.

for legal fees and imposes a mandatory (and variegated) levy on all recoveries.

As a civil justice design issue, the order in which third party funders can claim against any recovery can be a matter of debate. In Canada, the levy is received prior to the distribution of (typically settlement) funds to the class members. As a matter of principle, this order of distribution has been open to some criticism similar to the type based on traditional champertous grounds: that every penny placed in a third party funder's pocket is a penny taken from a class member. This is a matter left up to legislators and varies by jurisdiction. The other side of the coin is that most funded cases would not be advanced without such funding and that funders must be assured that their investments will yield adequate and predictable returns, lest they forgo such investments in future cases. In Ontario the governing recognition is that funders have provided significant funds and exposed themselves to high risks of adverse costs for which they should be duly rewarded in case of success. In the Competition Appeal Tribunal in England and Wales, by contrast, class members have the first opportunity to claim their damages in full, and funders may claim their share of the proceeds only from the unclaimed sums, which may disincentivize future funding in the long term.

Finally, although the availability of such funding options is clearly beneficial for prospective claimants and a boon to collective access to justice, this can also be beneficial for defendants, who are assured of recovery of any adverse costs awards. This is more true in the case of public funders, who provide full indemnification, than it is for commercial funders who may impose caps on their exposure to adverse costs. Given the economic realities of class actions, a jurisdiction that allows for either form of funding, whether public or commercial, or ideally both, will be better placed to fulfil the access to justice potential of such collective claims-making.

Conclusion

Interspersed in our discussion thus far has been the consistent importance placed on the rules governing fees and the costs of litigation. The three key economic enablers in a class action regime have been identified as the claimant (whether a class member or an ideological claimant, depending on standing rules), the class lawyer (whether a legal entrepreneur or, less frequently, a public interest actor), and the third party funder (whether a commercial entity or a public funder). Whether and to what extent any of these enablers play a leading or secondary role in advancing an action depends in large part on the costs and benefits of the action for each enabler and, by implication, the rules governing costs and fees. Some scholars have gone so far as to suggest that these rules are the most important facets of a regime. Rachael Mulheron has observed that 'costs and funding are at the root of all civil procedure', a situation that is exacerbated in the present context 'given the "forest fire" of resource-intensive, expensive, expert-reliant and lengthy litigation that most class actions invoke'.[66] When it comes to class actions, economic principles and criteria are ever-present parts of the discussion.

Although the economic barriers faced by claimants with mass justiciable problems are significant and have, to varying degrees, been cited as among the chief reasons why class actions can promote collective access to justice, there are also a host of non-economic barriers that such actions can help overcome. The wide range of class actions – from data breaches and environmental pollution to home care and child abuses and employment discrimination – and the often vulnerable and isolated people involved in such claims, shed light on some of these social and psychological reasons that traditional access to

---

[66] R. Mulheron, *Class Actions and Government* (Cambridge: Cambridge University Press, 2020) at 129.

justice research has detailed at length. These include past negative experiences with law and legal processes, differential legal consciousness, legal disempowerment and legal illiteracy. The common power imbalances involved in such actions, pitting powerful social and economic actors against groups of otherwise isolated individuals, can lead claimants to fear reprisals, especially in the workplace. The growth of sexual misconduct class actions against single perpetrators in the #MeToo era also signals that the social and psychological barriers associated with individual claims-making in such cases can be mitigated to an extent by procedures that collectivize claims and offer a certain strength-in-numbers for victims of abuse.[67]

This chapter has offered a framework for approaching class actions using a classical economic analysis of law approach, however recent forays in behavioural economics are also germane to the discussion. To the extent that law seeks to regulate behaviour, legislators must account for the ways in which people behave in response to rules.[68] Behavioural biases can also be overcome in a well-designed regime – and conversely, the design of a regime must account for such biases.

Notably, recent findings in experimental psychology indicate that individuals exhibit biases in favour of the status quo (the

---

[67] Although the phenomenon of absent class members – which refers to the reality that for most class actions nearly every class member is absent from the day-to-day activities of the proceeding, with the exception of the representative claimant and perhaps a few particularly active members – is often seen as a problem, there are also benefits to this phenomenon, particularly in cases like those arising out of the #MeToo movement, where victims/survivors do not need to experience the social and psychological pressures that may come with being active participants (and potential perceived re-victimization that may occur in sexual harm litigation).

[68] A. Sibony, 'A Behavioural Perspective on Collective Redress' in E. Lein, D. Fairgrieve, M.O. Crespo and V. Smith (eds), *Collective Redress in Europe – Why and How?* (British Institute of International and Comparative Law, 2015) at 49.

inertia bias).[69] Even where individuals have experienced justiciable problems, there is a behavioural bias towards inaction.[70]
This is especially pronounced where the justiciable problem is
a negative value claim. Such a preference for the 'default position' becomes important when legislators decide on whether
a class action regime should be implemented on an opt-in or
an opt-out model. From a behavioural perspective, an opt-out
regime would be optimal in accounting for the status quo bias
as a form of nudging for a desired policy outcome. This is not
unique to collective claims-making: for instance, retirement
plans benefit from increased participation where they proceed
on opt-out bases, as do organ donation rates.[71]

As we have seen, the collective access to justice gap is not
only a moral or legal problem, but can also be conceptualized in
economic terms as a social dilemma that needs to be solved. For
economists, that groups of individuals with justiciable problems
do not pursue their claims and recover their losses, due to these
claims being negative value, indicates a social inefficiency as
wrongdoers will not internalize the costs of their wrongdoing.
By allowing for collective procedures that aggregate these claims,
making them positive value and viable to pursue in court, the
justice system can contribute to solving this dilemma.[72]

---

[69] ibid at 51. See also W. Samuelson and R. Zeckhauser, 'Status Quo
Bias in Decision Making' (1988) 1 *Journal of Risk and Uncertainty* 7–59;
D. Kahnerman, J. Knetsch and R. Thaler, 'Anomalies: The Endowment
Effect, Loss Aversion, and Status Quo Bias' (1991) 5(1) *Journal of Economic
Perspectives* 193–206.

[70] This is often referred to in the access to justice scholarship as 'lumping it'.

[71] ibid (n 68) at 52. It is interesting that arguments against opt-out class
actions often take issue with the idea that a legal action can be advanced
without the active consent of class members – only passive consent is
necessary – and yet the opt-out mechanism is viewed as legitimate in
other areas that arguably have much greater significance to a person (than
a negative value claim), such as retirement planning and organ donation.

[72] Cost internalization involves a modicum of speculation and these costs
can in turn be passed down to customers or covered by insurance (which
may result in higher premiums).

FIVE

Conclusion

Over the past 20 years, class actions have proliferated globally to more than 35 states.[1] A basic lesson that this globalization of class actions has taught reformers is that legal transplants cannot be wholly adapted into new jurisdictions without accounting for differences in legal culture, history, and politics, including the role of litigation in democracy, the extent to which the use of private enforcement aligns with a state's regulatory governance framework, and the desirability of economically enabling private actors to pursue litigation for public goals. The proliferation of class actions does nevertheless reflect a recognition by policymakers of the need for new procedures to adequately protect groups of vulnerable people against powerful private (and public) entities. These are not, it must be reiterated, efforts to create new substantive rights, but rather simply to introduce procedural mechanisms to give effect to existing substantive law.

---

[1] Jurisdictions that have introduced some form of class or representative action over the past few decades, in addition to England and Wales, Australia, Canada, and the United States, include Argentina, Brazil, Chile, China, Denmark, Finland, Germany, Indonesia, Israel, Italy, Mexico, the Netherlands, Norway, Portugal, Russia, South Africa, Spain, Sweden and Taiwan, while other states and state formations have debated their adoption, including Austria, France, Poland and the European Union.

In recent years the empowerment of previously marginalized social groups has also contributed to the growth of an accountability culture in which holding wrongdoers to account through legal means has come to be viewed as a viable pathway to justice, particularly where established political channels of influence remain out of reach. Indigenous peoples, women, LGBTQ, racial and ethnic minorities, and disabled people have all deployed class actions as a means to advance their causes and access justice, whichever form this justice may take. In spite of attempts to portray such justice-seekers as engaging in abusive litigation motivated by easy money, such groups often do not (only) seek compensation for their incurred harms, but also public apologies, educational and medical programmes, cessation of wrongful activity, and social recognition of loss.

Despite this proliferation, however, and despite the recognition of the prevalence of collective justiciable problems, many states have introduced extensive 'brakes' or so-called 'safeguards' to limit the efficacy of the new procedures, based in no small part on fears of importing 'US-style class actions' and the successful lobbying efforts of corporate and defendant advocacy groups. These have included limiting class actions to a single sector, strict standing requirements, prohibitions on damages, and attacks on funding sources (notably third party funders). In England and Wales these 'brakes' have been a constant feature of proposed reforms.[2] Among these are restrictions on

---

[2] As noted earlier, fears of importing a US-style litigation culture in England and Wales are misplaced since, among other reasons, there are prohibitions on punitive damages, contingency fees, discovery, and the absence of civil jury trials. The criteria used in the certification test have also been disputed, especially in more mature First and Second Generation regimes. The approach taken in the Competition Appeal Tribunal is a conservative model that incorporates many brakes on prospective claims, including a preliminary merits test. This cautious approach is reflective of the tentativeness with which successive governments in the United Kingdom have approached collective actions.

contingency fee arrangements for class action lawyers, which has meant that third party funders are now the key economic enablers in this jurisdiction. In some ways, the future of class actions in England and Wales rests on how this industry will develop in the coming years, and the extent to which corporate lobby efforts to restrict its functioning will be successful. As this book has repeatedly pointed out, perhaps more than most areas of civil justice reform, the collective actions space is a field of contestation between competing social, economic and political forces.

The two major sticking points that have resurfaced in reform processes in England and Wales have been the opt-out model and the adoption of a generic procedure. A workable compromise has been sought on the first point whereby a class action can proceed on either an opt-in or an opt-out basis, subject to judicial discretion, although even here there has been fierce opposition to this compromise. On the second point, it has been a long-standing principle of civil justice dating back to the 1870s that procedure must be trans-substantive. That this principle was violated in the class action context is worrisome. It has had the effect of splintering efforts to implement the 'new procedures' that Lord Woolf advocated in his Final Report on Access to Justice in 1996 across the breadth of the substantive law. Now, instead of trade unions, human rights institutions, data protection and privacy groups, environmental organizations and other proponents uniting their efforts to promote change, each sector is left to its own devices in its respective area and the gestation period that is often necessary when a new regime is implemented must be endured independently, if and when each such area is reformed. Apart from competition law claims, the access to justice gap that Lord Woolf identified in 1996 remains for every other area of the law.

Interviews carried out for this research also suggested that the UK policy space has shifted to continuing reforms to legal aid provisioning and dealing with the ramifications of the

LASPO reforms, as well as Her Majesty's Courts and Tribunals Service's modernization programme and shift to online dispute resolution, with many stakeholders pessimistic about the prospect of major reforms in collective actions in the next five to ten years. The withdrawal of the United Kingdom from the European Union has also dented hopes that EU initiatives in this space would bring horizontal reforms to the collective action landscape in England and Wales.

Finally, among the challenges for proponents has been the relative neglect of class actions by access to justice researchers and reformers, as well as the broader diminishment of civil procedure in legal education in the United Kingdom. The access to justice paradigm continues to be largely individualistic, with few voices raising the pressing problems of collective justiciable problems, apart from a handful of civil proceduralists and the odd political scientist. It is hoped that this book will be a modest step towards encouraging scholars, reformers and practitioners in the field to engage more fully with class actions and collective access to justice in the coming years.

Methodological Note

This book is based on research conducted as part of a postdoctoral fellowship at the Bonavero Institute of Human Rights, University of Oxford, with the generous support of the Legal Education Foundation. The approach undertaken for this book has been a mixture of comparative procedural, political and historical analysis of the relevant regimes and economic analysis of the key enablers and incentives. The book draws on historical sources, case law, public statistics, parliamentary debates and a series of semi-structured interviews with civil justice stakeholders conducted over a one-year period between November 2018 and November 2019, with research ethics approval from the University of Oxford. In line with the impetus for writing this book, I have refrained from using more complex material (for example mathematical modelling in the economic framework, advanced statistics and the type of deep qualitative interview data more common to social science approaches) in favour of a 'light-touch' approach to ensure that the book is as readable and accessible as possible.

Index

Canadian Environmental Law
  Association 54
Cappelletti, Mauro 4, 17, 40
capping fees 36
care communities 54
case management 12, 13, 61, 62
catering assistants 68
cause of action 41
Celebrex 37
certification 11, 19, 32, 41, 42,
  47, 58, 72
Chamber of Commerce 112
champerty 109–10, 114, 117
chemical industry 37
child abuse 43, 44, 62, 116, 118
children 43, 54, 59, 76
Citizens Advice 73
Civil Justice Council 68, 69,
  83, 106
Civil Justice Review 1988 60
Civil Procedure Rules 6
Civil Proceedings Act 69
civil rights 30, 31, 35
Civil Rights Movement 4, 52, 80
claimants 61, 87, 95–100
claims on behalf of children 76
Clark, Baroness 28, 68
class actions 1, 2, 6, 18
  definition of 10–14
  economics of 87–94
  growth of 34–5
  politics of 49–55
  and workers 27
Class Actions Fairness Act
  2005 36
class arbitration 8
class of claimants 64
Class Proceedings Act 40, 41
Class Proceedings Fund 116
Coffee, John 36
Coke, Sir Edward 19
collective actions 59–65,
  66–70, 71–6
collective legal entity 26–8
collective redress 10, 13, 82
commercial activities 22, 26
commonality 11, 32, 41, 91
common law 20, 22, 24, 38, 39,
  51, 59, 61

'common sense' narratives 8, 56
compensation 82–5, 122
compensation culture 56, 69–70
compensatory damages 22
Competition Appeal Tribunal 14,
  28, 72, 74–5, 117
competition law 71, 103, 123
Competition Law Class Action 83
complex litigation 101
compulsory joinder 20
consent 75
Conservative Party/
  government 44, 70, 71, 77
consolidation 13, 59
Consumer Rights Act 2015 72
consumers 7, 52, 66, 72–3
contingency fees 72, 102–3, 104,
  106, 108
contraband 23
contraceptive implants 60
contracts 7, 25
copyright infringement 115
corporate abuses 52
corporate lobbies 15, 49, 73,
  85, 123
corporations 2, 19, 26, 32, 69, 89
cost internalization 89
costs 4, 6, 13, 44, 47, 89, 101,
  105, 108, 118
cost-shifting 53, 70, 72, 108
Court of Appeal 24, 76
Court of Chancery 21, 22
Covent Garden Market 23
Covington & Burling 33
credit card charges 115
Criminal Appeal Act 1907 4
Criminal Law Act 1967 111
criminal trials 4
cy-près 70, 83

D

damages 23, 24, 33, 53, 61,
  70, 117
  punitive 36, 58, 104, 122
Damages Based Agreements 103
data breaches 2, 62, 97
data protection 75–6, 123
Data Protection Act 1998 76
decision making 9, 13, 28